WHAT
You Say

WHEN
You Say

"I DO"

DEREK TRIPLETT

What You Say When You Say "I Do"
by Derek T. Triplett

© 2017 by Derek T. Triplett

For information, address:

The Church Online, LLC
1000 Ardmore Blvd.
Pittsburgh, PA 15221

International Standard Book Number: 978-1-940786-50-6

Library of Congress Catalogue Card Number: Available Upon Request

Printed in the United States of America

First Edition, April, 2017

Trademarks

Endorsements

"This is Derek Triplett at his finest! Gaining understanding is the principle thing and he has a profound grasp on relational issues. Long overdue, this is wisdom that will empower anyone who reads to get his or her relationship in divine order. Real, insightful, and transformative—this is one read that will revolutionize the way you approach love."

Michelle McKinney Hammond
Author of *Getting Real About Life, Love, and Men*

"Derek Triplett is an intellectual genius! This book will re-center and recapture the essence of one's ability to choose who they vow to in holy union."

Pastors Jathan and Veverly Austin
One Church Empowerment Center, Grand Rapids, Michigan

"Like only he can, Derek Triplett shares simple yet profound wisdom about the power of words, the power of intention, the power of choice, and the blessing of a healthy 'I DO.' This book will certainly be added to my list of required reading for couples in premarital counseling!"

Dr. Vikki Johnson
Chaplain, Speaker, Author, and Creator of Soul Wealth Academy

"Derek Triplett has hit a home run with this groundbreaking book that effectively prepares couples for marriage. His unique approach to the wedding vows and his commitment to healthy marital relationships are obvious. This is a must-have for ALL COUPLES."

Bishop John and Mrs. Sonjanique Guns
Founders of Your Marriage Matters

"Derek Triplett has done an outstanding job informing persons of what this thing called marriage is all about. This book breaks down what it means when persons recite their wedding vows. It is more than just for the ceremony—it's words to live by throughout the marriage. Having an awareness of the importance of vows prior to the ceremony will help persons make better choices."

Bishop Dwayne and Mrs. Carla Debnam
Morning Star Baptist Church, Baltimore, Maryland

"Derek is one of the 'best of the best' when it comes to relationship counseling. His insight into what makes couples tick is truly unique. His advice is always easy to understand, but comes across in a manner that breaks down our fragile ego walls. Every time I finish a discussion with Derek, I can truly say that I see things in a new light that instantly makes me better at being a husband and father."

John Brown
News Anchor/Talk Show Host

Table of Contents

SECTION
One

Who Wants To Be A Spouse?

A Case for Marriage

Why am I writing a guide to understanding the traditional marriage vows? Why another book on marriage for that matter? Well, the reason is simple: I am very pro-marriage, and I think marriage needs a little help these days.

I think that a good marriage is one of the greatest blessings God has given us to enjoy. The possible benefits derived from a great marriage are almost endless— for society, for the family, but especially, for the two individuals within the couple. I like that phrase, *the individuals within the couple*. It tells us that marriage is great not just in and of itself, but for each person within it. At the same time, the Bible says that marriage allows two people to become one. What a concept! What a miracle! Two people become one working unit that makes the individuals in the unit better. Wow!

Before we discuss marriage, though, I want to make a defense for singleness. In standing up for marriage, I am not saying that there is something wrong with you if you are single. Please do not read into what I am saying and assume that. I am not saying that a single person is in any way less than a happily married person. Too often, single people get the "You aren't married yet?" question from friends and family, as if being unmarried is somehow an undesirable state in which to live. Singleness is not an affliction; it is not a disease for which you are seeking a cure. It is also not a sentence that you are serving until you are paroled. If you are single, you should enjoy it and all of its benefits. Do not let people label you or pity you. And do not pity yourself.

Enjoy the freedoms of singleness. Focus on personal growth. Go where you want when you want. Get as many degrees as you desire. Pursue your career goals without any encumbrances. Serve your church and community as much as you choose. Marriage is filled with responsibility and obligation. As a single person, you control what you wish to give your time and attention to. That is some real freedom.

I know the benefits of singleness firsthand. I was married, then I was single for as long as I was married before I got remarried. Once I healed from the pain and trauma of my divorce, I learned to really enjoy being single for the reasons I mentioned before. For years, there was no pity party, no woe is me, and no desire or will to be married. I knew I did not need a wife. I needed a better me. I pursued healing and wholeness and enjoyed living my life without marital responsibility and accountability. I remember when an "old school" wife and mother asked me, "You're not married yet? Don't you need someone to take care of you?" My answers were "no" and "no." Marriage was not a need, and it never should be. For the complete person living the single life, marriage is change in category not an upgrade in the same category. Marriage makes life better for the person who is ready for it and wants the benefits and the responsibility. Otherwise, it just makes life different without necessarily making it better.

All that being said, marriage does offer some very significant personal, social, and spiritual advantages to a happily married person.

If a single person is healthy and whole, a good marriage can enhance their life and improve personal development. Now, I know there are plenty of romantic relationships between significant others in which some of the benefits I'm about to espouse can be attained, but I want to make it clear that I'm only promoting those benefits within the context of marriage. I am an old-school church guy who still believes in the principles the Bible teaches: that sex outside of marriage and cohabitation are wrong. Marriage has to come first. I believe that sex and living with your partner are a definite part of the full romantic relationship package. I just believe they should happen in the context of marriage in order to get the full benefit. Plus, it pleases God. However, if you don't agree, please keep reading anyway. This book is still full of good advice, even if we disagree on that fundamental point.

Which brings us back to the benefits of marriage. Whenever you try to sell a product, a concept, or as in this case, a way of life, you highlight its benefits and added value. Once again, I am not advocating that marriage is the only good, productive, and enjoyable way to live. I am simply promoting marriage as a great blessing from God with many unique advantages which more people could give a chance or even a second chance.

So, what are these advantages?

FOR THE INDIVIDUAL

A happy marriage makes each partner a better individual in several ways. First of all, it gives us an opportunity to fight our own proclivity to be selfish. As an individual, you are constantly tempted to give in to the propensity to be self-absorbed. That doesn't mean that selfishness is always bad or even avoidable. What I have learned over time is that the most giving people are still selfish in some way, and this isn't unique to those who give. We are all selfish on some level, no matter who we are.

This is immediately clear when we consider how we live. It is our privilege as adults to fashion our own lives as we see fit. We get to decide how we want to live, where we want to live, how and with whom we spend our time and resources. Individuality and personal freedom are hallmarks of the adult life. In other words, as adults, we get to be selfish about who we are and what we do.

Selfishness, though, can have some very negative consequences, particularly in modern life. We live in a culture where individualism seems to be king, and because of this, all indicators suggest that, as a society, we have lost our sense of the common good. There is still racial oppression, partisan politics, and an increasing gap between the haves and the have-nots. These exist and even increase because, as a culture, we have seemingly lost respect for human life. The murder rate in cities like Chicago is both mind-blowing and heartbreaking. The lead poison crisis in Flint, Michigan makes you wonder how a government can allow such things to happen to its citizens.

Stronger relationships can help fight against our society's modern, selfish indifference. Relationships cause us to be reminded that we are all puzzle pieces that connect with each other to complete a picture. Marriage, unlike any other relationship with the possible exception of parenthood, gives us reason, and even the requirement, to consistently put someone else's needs before our own. Selfish people usually do not fare well in marriage. If they do, their partner certainly does not. Successful marriage is about giving, sharing, compromising, and yielding on a daily basis. It forces us to break any patterns of being "me-first" or "me-only." That is personal improvement for any individual, and for society.

Secondly, marriage creates balance for the individuals in the couple. When you bring two people together who are necessarily different, they are able to contribute to each other's personal equilibrium. A spouse is an equal partner, and an equal can bring balance where we most need it. Nobody will know you like your spouse. They will know the good, the bad, and the ugly. They will know what you're best at and what you are not so good at. They will know what excites you and what annoys you. They will know what response various situations evoke from you. The right spouse knows when you need to chill and when you need to get it moving. In a good marriage, the spouses are complementary and supplementary to each other. Each knows how to offset their mate's weaknesses as well as help discover and develop strengths. What a gift!

> A spouse is an equal partner, and an equal can
> bring balance where we most need it.

A partner can also protect you from your extremes. That is such a relevant point, I think I have to repeat it: a partner can protect you from your extremes. We all have dominant traits that either work for us or against us. At times, we do not manage them well. The right spouse can help you with that. Men have dominant traits, as do women, and they differ. Our emotional makeup is different. Our decision-making patterns can differ. Gender is not the only difference. We all have prevailing beliefs and behavior patterns that are a condition of how we were raised. Men and women look at life differently. Just because those attributes exist and we are very connected to them doesn't mean we should not be rescued from them from time to time. A good spouse knows how and when to save you from yourself. What a blessing!

Marriage puts us in a situation where we have to learn to agree with another person. That's the reason some of you are not going to get married. I repeat, it puts you in a situation where you *have to* learn to agree with someone, which means you have to learn to negotiate. You must be able to give up some stuff, to sacrifice. You have to learn to see someone else's perspective. It puts you in a culture where you must learn to agree on the big stuff and the small stuff.

When you are perpetually single and living alone (SALA—let's see if that catches on), once you have fulfilled your job or business commitments, you are ruler of your time. You decide what you give attention to. You can spend your money how you please, see only the movies you want to see, etc., etc. Once you go home, you don't have to agree with anybody. You can watch whatever TV shows you want. The temperature in the house is going to be what you want it to be. If you don't want to clean up, you don't have to. You can eat what you want and when you want. There is no one you need to agree with while in your living space.

In short, the longer you are SALA, the more you get used to making unchallenged decisions and being able to dictate your time and dominate your space. This can be great in some ways, but it does leave room to grow as giving and thoughtful individuals.

After my divorce, I was SALA for a very long time. I was also a pastor and CEO of my church. Of course, there was submission to the Holy Spirit and consideration of others' opinions, thoughts, and perspectives, but in general, I was used to setting the dates, times, and agendas at work and at home. Unless my kids were home, I totally controlled my personal space. I got used to not having to agree. That put me totally out of balance. I am a better person now that I am back in balance and in a personal culture where it is not just my way. I have to consistently yield and agree. I must admit, the adjustment was at times a painful process, but I know it was for my good.

FOR RAISING CHILDREN

A healthy marriage provides the best environment to raise children. I'm not trying to judge anyone or raise the ire of any hardworking single parent. My house is glass, and I collect no stones. There are some single moms and dads who are putting in amazing work raising their children. I am saying that a good marriage sets the most optimal home environment to raise children. The same gender differences discussed earlier come into play here as well. A male parent is a male parent. A female parent is a female parent. Before you close the book or skip to the next section, please hear me out. I'm not saying dumb things that fall into the category of "a dad can't teach a daughter how to do hair" or "a mom can't teach a son how to shoot a jump shot." I am saying that, generally speaking, male and female perspectives and behavior patterns differ. Children who are raised in a good two-parent home get the benefit of the balance of complementary viewpoints. Children need to be mothered and fathered. Each one pours different qualities into the child that help make them who they will become. No matter how great the mother is, children miss some aspects of their molding and shaping if they are missing a father. The same is true if they are missing a mother.

I have great children. They are tremendous young adults. I am a great father. Their mom is a great mother. The wonderful thing about our family is, despite divorce, we were never enemies and our children were always the first priority. Whatever else was going on took a back seat to us raising our children together. Even during and after separation and divorce, we effectively co-parented. Our children needed both of us to become who they have become.

One of the things I told my children when they came of age was that their marriages needed to work, and so they needed to pray, date effectively, and choose wisely. They were used to the benefit of parents who sacrificed and kept the family unit together during their developmental years despite divorce. Birthdays and holidays were spent together. We attended their games and school events as a family. They pretty much spent time with both of us on a daily basis. I did not want them to think that our behavior was normal. We showed them what great divorced parents looked like, but what we did not show them was how to have a good marriage that lasted. I wish we had because divorce or single parenting makes an already difficult task so much more difficult.

One of the reasons for this is that time is such a major factor for divorced and single parents. Generally speaking, single parents are often too busy to concentrate fully on the needs of their children. Raising children is a grind! Children require a lot time, attention, and effort. Every parent needs some time off. If they are the only involved parent, or the other parent is far away, who relieves them? When a parent is fatigued, the child can be neglected. I am not even speaking about the type of neglect that is arrest-worthy. I am speaking of the child not getting enough of that attention, care, discipline, and supervision. I am speaking of the child having to be kept occupied by television and video games because the parent is at work or just too tired to spend the time doing something more productive with their child. The child suffers, especially when there is no extended family around to take up the slack.

Children have to be raised, and raising them requires a huge investment of time. I have talked with so many single mothers who have the same complaint: since having their kids, they have no life. The children demand practically all of their time and energy because there is no equal partner to share the responsibility and the load. The idea of "first comes love, next comes marriage, then comes the baby carriage" is not just a matter of morality or religion. Marriage gives some much-needed help with the children. Mom and Dad are the tag team champions of raising kids. Juggling multiple children with different activity schedules, including feeding times, babysitting, play dates, homework, class projects, discipline, internet monitoring, cell phone monitoring, and the like all can be shared by two parents. Two is better than one.

FOR THE PERPETUATION OF THE INSTITUTION

A final argument that I would like to proffer in my case for marriage is directed to the Christian church, particularly the urban Christian church. We have to shine a better light on marriage. Too many young people do not think it is something they want to do, in many cases because they have not seen it work. This perpetual singleness we have in the black church is negatively affecting the next generation. The future stewards of the church in many cases want nothing to do with marriage.

Personally, I think marriage is the greatest thing God gave us to experience outside of salvation. A happy marriage is a blessing from God and can be an important contributor to a great life. I love church, but I think life ought to be better than the church experience. I love corporate worship and fellowship with the saints, but I have seen too many people who are somewhere between bored and miserable outside of church activities. I don't think your happiest moments should be in church. I don't think your most joyful moments should be in church. I think your happiest moments should be within the context of living the life God has given. We cannot just preach and exhort on this subject. We have to model what great marriage looks like if we are going to get the next generation to seek it at a greater rate than they presently are.

> I think your happiest moments should be within the context of living the life God has given.

The research on this subject is easy to find. We always talk about the statistic that, in America, 50 percent of first marriages end in divorce. That trend is beginning to change, but the numbers can be misleading. The divorce rate is dropping, but the marriage rate is dropping at a similar pace. So, it's not really that fewer people are getting divorced, it's that fewer people are getting married in the first place. Fewer people are getting married because they do not believe in the institution or the necessity of it for their exclusive, romantic relationships. Either that, or they are afraid of it.

Fornication and cohabitation are not taboo anymore. They are now the cultural norm. At the time of this writing, it is the day after the announcement that Angelina Jolie has filed for divorce from Brad Pitt. I do relationship segments for a local Orlando news station. After the "Brangelina" divorce was announced, my producer called me in to do a segment centered on their breakup. They have been together for 12 years and married two years. They have six children together. Three of them are adopted. They lived together and built a family for 10 years before getting married. There was no critique of their family choices because it is the norm. Marriage is simply no longer viewed as a relationship necessity in the American culture. This, in part, is responsible for the drop in the marriage rate. The moral standard has basically been erased. I am saying, as Christians, we should re-raise the standard.

The move away from marriage is not just because of loosening morals. It is also because of a fear of marriage. People just do not think it works. The cynics will cite the Brad and Angelina story as "proof," using the short time they were married as evidence. Some would hypothesize that the relationship was fine for a decade until they got married. Marriage destroyed their relationship. Right? I have spoken with people who mention stories like this so they can say, repeatedly, they just do not want to try marriage because it just does not work. Wow! The blessing of marriage is viewed as the easiest way to curse a perfectly good relationship. They believe that divorce is basically inevitable, so to elude breakups, they avoid marriage.

Unfortunately, that is a very understandable reaction. Imagine growing up never seeing a happily married couple. What adolescents see helps to shape what they expect from adulthood. Look around using the lens of a teen if you can. If all you see are single people, unmarried or cohabiting couples, and divorcees who willingly tell you their horror stories about being married, how would that shape your perspective of marriage and your desire to jump the broom? I think the effect is tremendous. The average teenager now does not have a goal of getting married. That used to be at the top of the list in previous generations. It may not be in the top five anymore. According to information released by Pew Research Center (2014), 25 percent of millennials are likely to never be married. Pew Research has also predicted that more people under 35 will be single throughout their lifetimes than at any other time in history.

A *New York Post* article by David Kaufman (2016) found that, when millennials do think of marriage, they have specific thoughts about redefining it:

> For whether they call it a "starter" marriage, "beta" marriage or "test" marriage, the 25- to 35-year-old generation has a far more elastic definition of the concept of "forever." How elastic? A recent study found that 43 percent of millennials supported a form of marriage that allowed couples to easily split up after two years, while a full third were open to "marriage licenses" valid—like mortgages—for set periods of time. ("Millennials' latest mistake: embracing the 'starter marriage'")

Wow! The fear of marriage is real. It has set in. Many have concluded that forever is a fantasy and impossibility. They have never seen it happen with anyone they are connected with, so they don't believe it can last. This is a clear case of hopelessness. Christians need to help restore society's belief in marriage. How? Firstly, we do it by advocating the blessings and benefits of marriage as I have attempted to do in this chapter. Secondly, and more important, we do the work to make "…and they lived happily ever after" an incarnational reality in our own lives. We can increase the marriage rate and decrease the divorce rate in present and future generations if we become living proof that marriage works.

I love seeing couples celebrate 30, 40, and 50 plus years of marriage. It is a fantastic thing to see. The effect these occurrences can have on young people's belief in marriage can be tremendous. People are more apt to believe in what they see rather than what they hear about. If more children begin to see loving, functional couples in their homes, it will counteract the negative noise that is heard so often concerning marriage. What a difference it would be if more kids could say, "I want what my parents have."

> If more children begin to see loving, functional couples in their homes, it will counteract the negative noise that is heard so often concerning marriage.

Now, millennials are not the only age group avoiding marriage. I am a part of Generation X. I hear so many of my peers opine negatively about the institution of marriage. I do not think it is coincidental that many of them are divorced or never married. They passionately and boldly make the statement that marriage does not work or it is just not for them.

I remember having this discussion in a church Bible study. While teaching, I made a comment concerning marriage. Someone stated, "I'm never getting married." I responded, "You do understand that when you say you are going to be single for life that you are also saying that you are going to be celibate for the rest of your life." I can still remember the look on the woman's face. Her expression said that was not what she was saying. We are so conditioned by society and driven by our own desires and will that we either subconsciously forget or consciously ignore that God intended for sex to be enjoyed within the bounds of marriage. Regardless of the cultural norms, any sex outside of marriage is out of bounds. Not everybody needs sex in their lives. So, if that is your spiritual, emotional, and physical disposition, then marriage is of no benefit to you in this area.

For the rest of us, though, we need to make sure sex once again becomes tied to marriage. We need to make sure marriage stops being a scary word to young people. To do that, we have to start demonstrating all the positive ways marriage can shape our lives: for the good of ourselves, our families, our society, and our faith.

REVIEW

1. Summarize the reasons marriage should still be important for us, despite how little interest society places in it today.

2. How has the breakup of "Brangelina" or other celebrity marriages helped to erode the idea of marriage?

3. How should you be using your time when you are single?

4. Why is it our responsibility as Christians to improve the image of marriage through our own actions?

SOUL SEARCHING

1. Summarize your own past experience with singleness and marriage. Include your thoughts on the marriages you have seen around you. How have negative experiences turned you against the idea of marriage?

2. How can you counteract these negative associations to start seeing all the blessings marriage offers?

3. Have you done enough personal growth on your own to enter marriage as a happy and complete person and partner? If not, what can you do to complete that growth now?

4. Why does God want us to keep sex within the marital relationship?

Good Dating, Bad Dating

Usually, there are at least a few dates before there is a wedding. I have heard of love at first sight, but marriage at first sight is a little much, even if television did dream up a show where people do get married at first sight.

Most normal people date as a precursor to marriage. So, that leads to a very important question: are you good or bad at dating? I do not mean are you good at getting dates or do you have good dates. The question is: do you date in a way that gives you the type of experiences that provide you with the necessary knowledge to make a good choice in a relationship that leads to marriage?

Relationships are a choice; more specifically, they are a decision. Good decisions are based on good, available data and information. Proper dating helps you get that data and information. So, again, are you good or bad at dating?

During the week of Valentine's Day, I usually talk about love and relationships on my radio show. A couple of years ago, the topic was "Cupid or Stupid." I know, it sounds a little harsh, but it allowed me to discuss with my audience the importance of being wise in relationships. Some people just aren't. They are hopeless romantics looking for their soulmate. They believe that, ultimately, cupid is going to strike with one of his arrows, and they will live happily ever after without any work or decision-making at all. I am a romantic as well, but I know that a good relationship with the right person is not magic. It is not simply a matter of praying and waiting on God either. You have to do the work. While you are enjoying the date, do the work. As you are enjoying the gifts, do the work. When you are basking in the feelings of butterflies in your stomach, do the work. The work will pay off in the end.

What work should you be doing during the dating season? You should be acquiring the requisite information in order to make a good relationship choice. Francis Bacon said, "Knowledge is power." The Bible says, *"My people are destroyed from lack of knowledge"* (Hosea 4:6, NIV). Kool Moe Dee said, "Knowledge is king." (Wow, Bacon, Bible, and Moe Dee. I ran the gamut on that one.) The point is, during the dating process, you need to be learning as much as you can about your mate, yourself, and the mix of the two of you.

WHO IS THIS PERSON YOU ARE DATING?

"Let's get to know each other" is a common phrase in dating. Getting to know someone is crucial in developing a deeper relationship. Scripture teaches that people look at the outer appearance, but it is the heart that really matters. That is not to say that physical attraction is not important, because it is. It is just one factor though and is ultimately not the most important. The heart matters most. Who is this person sitting across from you at the core of their being? That is the information you are after. What are their spiritual beliefs? How are those beliefs practiced? What is their personality type? What is their position on the battle of sexes? How do they view the role or function of each gender? What are their political views? How about their views on money matters? Are they confident or do they have self-esteem issues? How do they interact with family and the public in general? Are they outgoing or introverted? What's their work ethic? How do they handle conflict? Are they clean or not so much? Do they have OCD? Are they communicative? The list goes on.

The answers to these questions are needed to make good choices in relationships. It takes time, interaction, and conversation to gain the knowledge you need and discover the truth you require to decide if this person is right for you. Again, it takes work, even while you're having fun. Now, if you are going to spend the rest of your life with a person, you will always be enrolled in the school of your mate. It will be a lifelong learning process. But effective dating should give you the basic knowledge needed to make a decision about whether you want to pursue a major in that relationship's future.

Conversation is pivotal. Real talk is paramount. No, I'm not talking about interrogation on the first few dates. But, you need to talk for real. At some point, surface conversation only leads to superficial knowledge and a shallow relationship. A shallow dating relationship can lead to deep marital problems. Occasionally, if not often, people can have a romance they enjoy so much that they claim their passion is enough to ensure their relationship's future without any mutual soul-searching with their partner. The truth is, though, once they have zeroed in on the sound of wedding bells, they protect the relationship from anything that could jeopardize it, even reality and truth. Real talk about real issues ceases. No one wants to have a conversation that could rock the boat. This is a bad choice. You cannot protect the future of a relationship from its present. Do not let wedding bells make you a dumbbell. Learn. Pray. Decide. You need to know who your partner is. You have to keep talking.

Information isn't just discovered through conversation, however. It also comes through experience and interaction. There is a biblical principle that basically states that God is revealed in context. Revelation requires a situation. The same is true when getting to know a person. Varied experiences will reveal the nature of a person. It is usually a mistake to date in a limited context that does not afford varied experiences. Most of us have seen one of the many versions of the movie where two people of the opposite sex are stranded on a deserted island and end up falling in love. I can tell you, almost with absolute certainty, after they are rescued, the relationship does not last. Their love developed under very specific conditions, and without those specific conditions, there was no relationship left.

Have you ever known people who were in a clandestine relationship (side chick or side dude) that ultimately led to them becoming each other's one and only? In many cases, the relationship fails because they now share more than a few scattered moments together without any outside intrusion. The broader context of a full, legitimate relationship reveals the holes in the connection.

That is why it is important to vary your experiences in the dating process. There is only so much you can learn about a person with a constant relationship diet of the same experiences. Are you doing the same things on your dating activity register over and over again? Is it dinner and a movie or lunch at the same few restaurants again and again? Is it go to church together, have lunch, and text later over and over? Different situations show the different sides of a person. How is she with just the two of you versus when around a group of people? How is he with his friends in contrast to with your friends? Does she react differently in outdoor, casual events than she does with indoor, more formal events? How does he handle it when you are the center of attention? How does he handle you when he is the center of attention? How does she treat you when she is under stress? Does he remain communicative when he is under stress? Does she find a way to enjoy a favorite activity of yours that is not one of hers? Have you seen enough to know that he respects women in general and not just the one he is dating? The list goes on. It will take time to learn the answers to all these questions with your potential partner, but you cannot learn much while doing the same things you always do.

WHO ARE YOU?

Dating relationships are also a great way to learn more about yourself, if you use them correctly. Often, you have to be in a relationship to discover what you truly need in a relationship. Of course, we learn about ourselves through contemplation, self-analysis, and reflection. It is important to examine yourself and draw conclusions about likes and dislikes, needs and wants.

> Often, you have to be in a relationship to discover what you truly need in a relationship.

I remember when my daughter was about 14. Though she was not allowed to date until 16, I asked her to make a list of the qualities a young man needed to have in order for her to consider dating him. I wanted her to think and contemplate who she was, who she wanted to be, and then consider the sort of person she wanted to date. That way, she would have something to fall back on as a basis for her decision, other than he was cute and interested. She comprised the list. I do not know if she ever used it, but I hope I taught a principle. You have to know who you are in order to know what you want or need. Some of that knowledge you can pick up just thinking ahead, like my daughter did, but some cannot be gained in isolation. You have to "go live."

"Going live" is sports terminology. In football or basketball, the coach teaches a play she wants the team to run. She walks the team through it. Once the team has learned the rudiments of the play and what each player is supposed to do, they run the play at full speed without any opposition. After that is completed a few times successfully, the coach announces, "Let's go live." That means running the play against the opposing defense or offense in live action to see if the team can execute. To discover who you are and what you like, need, and want in a relationship you eventually need to be in one. You have to go live. Again, situations give revelation. You can learn a lot about yourself while experiencing how someone else chooses to treat you.

You can discover how much attention you require within a relationship when your partner is giving you more or less than you need. You can pick up on how much alone time you really need once you start sharing your time with someone else. You can identify pet peeves once something someone does starts to get on your nerves. You can identify something you enjoy once a partner introduces it to you. You can unearth hidden parts of your personality once the relationship draws them out. Dating properly can help you learn so much about yourself, if you are willing.

THE MIX AND MATCH

My wife made her first 7UP pound cake the other day. It was light and delicious. That is a pretty amazing accomplishment for her first try. I have never baked a pound cake, but I have tasted my share of bad ones at church events. They were not so light and something other than delicious. My wife got the recipe online. She said the key to the cake turning out so well was to simply follow the instructions *precisely* on how the ingredients should be mixed. The recipe was very specific about that.

I love good music and great sound. Years ago, I went to a recording session in Jacksonville, Florida. The choir was amazing. The songs were well-composed. The band was awesome. As we would say, they were killing it. Sometime later, when the album was released, I was so disappointed. It was not what I expected. What I heard in the recording session did not transfer to tape. The house mix was not what went to tape. Great music, bad mix.

Here is one last story to present my point. My first job out of college was with Procter & Gamble. I had interned with them the summer of my junior year, and they subsequently offered me a full-time position. Among the many things that stood out during that interview process was a statement the interviewer made. "We are a great company. Judging by your resume, you seem like a good candidate. We are going to find out in this interview if we are a match." Two variables can have individual goodness, even greatness. The question remains whether they are a good match.

I said earlier that dating is preparatory, and it should be used to gather the information needed to make an informed decision about whether or not to pursue a marital relationship. A part of that prep work is to determine if two people mix and match well. It is quite possible that two good individuals need to stay as far away from each other as they can. Have you ever heard the phrase, "They look good on paper"? You can put the personal profiles of two individuals side-by-side and conclude they would make a perfect couple. They just might, or they could be a disaster waiting to happen. Do they mix well? Are they a good match? You can only learn that by putting the two people together in and room and seeing how they interact.

Partners in a good relationship will complement and, when necessary, supplement each other. They are two pieces of the same puzzle rather than two slices of the same pie. Different slices of the same pie have the same ingredients, consistency, temperature, etc. They only differ in size and weight. Put any two pieces of the same pie together, and they'll fit, since they are the same exact thing. That's not how people work. They are different in many ways, and to work as a couple, they have to find a way to fit together. That's why I prefer to think that the individuals within the couple are different pieces of the same puzzle. You remember those jigsaw puzzles with the giant pieces from elementary school, don't you? The individual pieces contained some of the same elements, a portion of the whole picture. Each piece is oddly shaped so as to only interlock with other specific pieces. When they are correctly fitted together, you can see the complete picture. When they are not, the picture is a mess and the pieces won't fit. In fact, you can break the pieces by trying too hard to force them together.

The individuals within the couple are not identical. That is why they have to first be complementary. Too many people fall for the opposites attract cliché. Yes, opposites can attract, but total opposites find it difficult staying together. Healthy, long-lasting relationships usually require two different people who have found common ground. Each person brings different elements to the relationship that add value to their partner. A great partner is a good complement to who you are. Like the right shirt and tie complement a nice suit, like the right pair of shoes complements a beautiful dress, the individuals within the couple do not simply accessorize, they complete.

Additionally, the individuals within the couple may have to supplement each other. They may have to help provide something that is missing within their partner. It is a wonderful, beautiful, liberating thing when a person knows his limitations and inabilities. And yes, we all have limitations and inabilities. It is great when you find a partner who can pick up your slack. Have you watched any of the recent Avengers or X-Men movies? The heroes do not just complement each other; they supplement each other. They each have unique powers that their partners do not have. They use those powers to assist each other. When couples have the right mix and the individuals within the couples are the correct match, each has access to, and benefits from, the gifts, skills, abilities, and even anointing he/she does not possess.

> When couples have the right mix and the individuals within the couples are the correct match, each has access to, and benefits from, the gifts, skills, abilities, and even anointing he/she does not possess.

That is an excellent by-product of being in a good relationship. The dating process mines for the potential gold of a good relationship. When used correctly, it is thorough enough for a person to not get tricked by fool's gold.

REVIEW

1. Why is it important to date well?

2. What sort of things should you learn about your partner while dating? How do you make sure you keep learning new things?

3. What can you learn about yourself from dating?

4. Why are we more like puzzle pieces than pieces of pie?

SOUL SEARCHING

1. Are you, or were you, a good dater? How can you improve your dating technique to find a better partner? Or, if you are married, how can you use the techniques in this chapter to get to know yourself and your partner better and become a better match?

2. How much do you know about your partner? Or, how much did you know about your last partner? Could you answer all the questions asked in this chapter before you were considering marriage or breaking up?

3. What do you need to make a good "mix" with your personality? What about you needs to be supplemented by a partner? What benefits do you bring to your partner or potential partner?

Three

A Case for Marriage Prep

I have a question. Why is it so easy to get married? I know it is not an easy decision to make, and wedding planning can be as fun as a root canal, but I'm talking about the act of getting married. Yes, the government sanctions the marriage license, but why is it so easy to exchange vows and be named husband and wife? In this country, getting married is one of the easiest things to do. Getting married is easier than getting a driver's license. It is easier than becoming a real estate agent, a dental hygienist, or a high school basketball or football referee. Referees have to be certified. Who certifies a person to be a husband or wife? All you need to do to get married is want to get married and find a partner who does as well. There is no sanctioning body and no preparation required. If you meet the legal standards, no one can deny your pursuit to be a husband or a wife. You can get married just because you want to.

Imagine the state of the medical field if you could be sanctioned as a physician by paying a fee, having a ceremony, and having someone pronounce you as a doctor. How many more traffic fatalities would there be if you didn't have to pass a proficiency test to get your driver's license? You get my point. When something is serious, there is some level of preparation and/or certification involved. Yet, most of us go into marriage, the most significant human relationship, with very little preparation. The easiest places to get married in the United States are Las Vegas and the state where I reside, Florida. I find it very ironic that some states, such as Kansas and Utah, are making it more difficult to get a divorce but have not significantly increased the prerequisites for getting married. Louisiana, Arizona, and Arkansas, on the other hand, have at least made an effort to increase the preparation for marriage as well as decrease the divorce rate by becoming covenant marriage states. With a covenant marriage, premarital counseling is required and there are limited grounds for divorce. Couples also have to seek counseling to save their marriage before a divorce is granted.

> When something is serious, there is some level of preparation and/or certification involved. Yet, most of us go into marriage, the most significant human relationship, with very little preparation.

I am a staunch proponent of premarital preparation, but it should be serious preparation. I don't just mean dating well, either. That's a great start to making sure you are getting closer to the right person, but there is more work to be done before you tie the knot with that person for life.

I was 22 when I got married the first time. I went through three premarital counseling sessions from three different pastors, each lasting an hour or less. We were given certain scriptural verses. You know the ones. We got some helpful hints on household management. There was talk about how important my ministry was, and we were told to keep God first, pray, and love each other. Those sessions did next to nothing to prepare us for the life we were about to undertake.

They all did their best, I guess, but I wish I had been more prepared. In the end, I failed miserably, the marriage failed—though it was not for lack of trying—and so much damage was done.

Each time I do my premarital coaching sessions, it is a bit troubling because the things I teach now are the things I wish I had known. If I had known the lessons I embrace and teach now, I never would have ended up the way I did. My first marriage would have never become a divorce statistic. With my own experience in mind, then, I make sure my premarital sessions are extremely thorough. I decided that effectively preparing people for marriage would be one of my contributions to the kingdom of God and to the world.

My premarital coaching course is a nine-hour course that covers subjects that are critical to the success of marriage. When offered in my home church, the couples cannot send invitations or publicize a wedding date until completion of the course. It is easier to step back or step away if invitations have not been sent, after all. The curriculum is a prep course to be used as a tool to determine if they are ready for marriage. It is not a "helpful information" class for those who are planning to get married. Most people go on to have happier, better marriages, but not all. There are those who take the course and decide they are not ready. Some people, though, go through with the ceremony just to avoid embarrassment. Somehow, in our culture, going through a divorce is considered less embarrassing than calling off a wedding. Go figure.

I focus so much on premarital coaching because a marriage ending badly is so devastating, despite what our culture says. When you are married with children and the marriage fails, there can be extensive negative repercussions. There can be emotional, financial, and even spiritual injury. I intentionally use the word "injury" to differentiate it from pain. Divorce is certainly painful. It HURTS. Dealing with the pain is difficult, but with time, prayer, and many times therapy, the pain eventually subsides and finally goes away. The injuries, on the other hand, can remain for years, even after adjustments are made and life gets better. I presently have a great life, but occasionally, I still have to deal with a nagging injury from a previous time.

Children can be injured as well. They are more resilient than we expect (thank God), but that doesn't mean they walk away from their parents' divorce unharmed. The generational effect has been well-documented. In their book, *The Unexpected Legacy of Divorce* (2001), Wallerstein, Lewis, and Blakeslee document a 25-year study of children who are victims of divorce. The effects of divorce surfaced in their self-perception, approach, and outlook on relationships 25 years later. Not only did the children go through the pain of the divorce at the time, their adult lives were also affected. Divorce is the terrible gift that keeps on giving.

Many people know that I jokingly call myself a bootlegged sociologist. I have never taken a single course in sociology, but I was a pastor for over 25 years and have worked hard to address the social ills that plague my community and this country. My experiences and my reading cause me to ask questions, form hypotheses, and draw conclusions. It is my elementary opinion that much of what is wrong in the black community can be tied back to the disintegration of the black family. This opinion is in no way novel. Preventing broken homes will help prevent other entities and institutions from breaking. When marriages fall apart, homes are broken. This brokenness can bleed into other areas and cause the breaking to spread into our neighborhoods, schools, and even our churches. Happy marriages are not just a nice thing to have in the black community. They are critical.

I know there is a plethora of issues that need to be addressed in communities, like poor housing and schools, food deserts, crime, poverty, and unemployment. Yet, better families could be a catalyst for improvement in these areas. Now, I am sure there are sociological studies that analyze the cause and effect relationship between family breakdown and these other variables. Nevertheless, we may not be able to destroy systems and structures meant to cripple certain groups, but we can begin to address the issue of broken homes, which is a problem of epic proportion. A great place to start is better premarital preparation. It just makes sense to put in the work to prepare for something that has a generational impact.

The average time to plan a wedding is between six and 18 months. The median cost of a wedding in the United States is just under $27,000. That is the time and money spent to prepare for a wedding day. It is not even an entire day. Most weddings take 45 minutes or less, and most receptions last about three hours. If you add an hour for pictures, the entire production is less than six hours. In contrast, many couples spend very little time, if any, in intentional, structured premarital preparation for the most significant human relationship that is supposed to be for life. We need to reverse those priorities.

REVIEW

1. What are some of the social problems that stronger marriages might help alleviate?

2. How much time do most couples spend in premarital preparation?

3. Why is divorce the terrible gift that keeps on giving?

SOUL SEARCHING

1. How long do you think you should spend in premarital prep before you decide to go through with the marriage?

2. What questions would you like to see addressed in premarital prep?

3. How could more preparation make for stronger and longer marriages? How could this help with some of society's lingering issues?

Oh Wow! A Vow!
The Power of Your Promise

"Do you promise?"

I do not like answering that question. Don't get me wrong. I am a person who values keeping my word. I just do not like saying the words "I promise." I rarely say them. I just tell people, "I will be there," "I will get it done," or "I have got you, don't worry." Sure, it may be semantics. I make promises. I just do not call them promises. I really don't like saying the words. I cringe when someone demands I do.

This is not a random quirk. My feelings and disposition are residuals from a previous period of my life. I am a divorcee. That means, I broke the most important promise I ever made, and the consequences were catastrophic. God has healed, blessed, and made it possible to recover, but my past failure created a reticence that I still carry with me (this is just one of the injuries mentioned in the last chapter that I still carry with me). A promise creates a direct link between what I am saying now and what I am going to do in the future. I do not like making promises that guarantee action that has to be performed over a long period of time. I now truly understand the responsibility a major promise can create. So, I do not make promises often.

Part of my reticence is because the promise I broke was a particularly powerful one. A vow is a special type of promise. By definition, it is an earnest promise. It is a solemn pledge to live a prescribed way, performing predetermined responsibilities and meeting particular expectations. A vow is a declaration that something will be done. It is a promise to perform. When you make a vow to someone, you are making a personal promise to contribute to help shape the actual events of the present and future for that person. It is a verbal agreement. To break a vow is a breach of contract. To make a vow you have no intention of keeping is perjury and fraud.

MARRIAGE VOWS

The marriage vows may be the most serious of all vows. First, you are making promises to another individual and to God. Secondly, the marriage vows are meant to be a lifelong commitment. Very few promises have the phrase "until death" tied to them. That is forever. What you say at the marriage altar is supposed to be in effect until they roll your body down the church aisle and place your casket at that same altar again. It is a public declaration as well, especially if you have a formal wedding with guests. Preachers say, "We are gathered here in the sight of God and these witnesses." The couple feels so strongly about what they are about to say that they choose to say their vows in front of a bunch of people. You invite people to come hear you make promises to each other. Now, I know most people do not think of wedding ceremonies in those terms. It's more about the love, the pageantry, and the emotion. But, everything in the ceremony leads up to the exchanging of the vows, so, in essence and in truth, couples invite people to watch and listen to them make promises to each other.

That promise comes with quite a price tag, and not just for the couple. Attending a wedding can be expensive. Some people have travel expenses, food and lodging, plus the cost of a wedding gift. There is also the sacrifice of time. Most formal weddings are on weekends. People give up their weekend to witness loved ones make a lifelong commitment to each other. As a pastor for almost 30 years, I gave up numerous Saturdays in order to perform weddings.

For all that, I have only attended a couple of weddings that I was not officiating. I have only been a groomsman twice in my life. I was always involved in the promise side of things, which turns out to be the cheaper side. Some of you ladies have had the expensive pleasure of being a bridesmaid, attendant, or usher in a wedding on several occasions. How many bridesmaid dresses do you have that you can't wear anywhere else? In all my years of performing weddings, I've only seen a few cute bridesmaid dresses. They are usually ugly. Come on. Some of you all have four or five of them hanging in the closet that you will never wear anywhere else. Oh, you probably have a few pairs of shoes that fit the same description too. You gave up a Friday night for the rehearsal and all day Saturday. You paid the cost of hair, nails, etc. You dealt with the moment when your great friend that you love had a bridezilla moment. You loved being there for your girl, and maybe you don't think about your time and money when the couple finalizes their divorce, but you'd have every right to feel aggrieved. After all, you spent all that time and money to witness a promise that your friend wasn't willing to follow through on. People get legitimately upset for much less.

The expenses aren't that much lighter on the men's side. A few years ago, my best friend, John Guns, got married. It was my honor to be his best man. He and is wife Sonjanique are a terrific couple. To participate in the wedding, I had to drive to Pensacola, Florida. That was an almost 10-hour drive. There were expenses for lodging and meals in addition to the tuxedo rental. I do not like rented tuxedos, and I abhor rented formal shoes. I own two tuxedos but had to rent another to be uniform. At the wedding, my daughter said to him, "My daddy must really love you for him to be in a rented tux because that is not him." I told John that they better work, and if they didn't make it, I wanted my money back. It was a joke, of course, but there was some truth behind it: if you make your loved ones go to so much work, you better mean what you promise.

Oh, by the way, John did the same thing for me a few years later. He was right there as I took my vows. It was a great day, and I married a great lady. Nevertheless, I still remembered that I was taking the vows *again*. I was, and am, grateful to God for a second chance, but I am still very conscious of my failure to live up to a previous commitment and to keep an earlier promise made in the sight of God and witnesses. It made me doubly committed to getting this promise—said in front of John and all my family and friends—right for life.

All of this expense and effort is worth it because marriage vows are a complete set of promises that are meant to govern the person you will be and the things you will and will not do. That's a big deal, and it's worth celebrating in a big way. The promises exchanged at the altar say to your spouse (in front of all those witnesses), "This is what you can bank on from me for the rest of your life." They are your commitment to help create a specific ongoing reality for you and your partner. They are words that are meant to shape your existence. One of the most important consequences of taking the marriage vows is that the promises made create an expectation and become the primary fixed, foundational element in both of your lives.

When you take the marriage vows, a new world is created for both spouses. When you give yourself to someone in marriage, all individual life decisions are then affected by the marriage. Marriage creates new contexts and new constraints. When you agree to marry, your partner now begins to make decisions about his or her life based on the promise you made them. You affect their choices concerning their life. They established new boundaries in every other relationship because of a promise you made. They cut off some relationships based on the promises you made. Based on your promises at the altar, there are things they don't even consider now. They base their life choices on the promises you made.

> When you take the marriage vows,
> a new world is created for both spouses.

Consider this: there is a dream job your spouse wants, but he/she doesn't take it because it is in a city that is not good for both of your career paths. Or, there is an old friend your spouse is fond of, but you don't get along with them, so your spouse slowly cuts them off. These situations are perfectly natural and correct because your spouse is living in a new world, one with boundaries secured by your promise. In this new world, your concerns have to be weighed in everything, just as their concerns have to be weighed in all your decisions. That's a radical new way to live after you say "I do." There's a lot of weight to those words!

So much sacrifice of our personal selfishness is acceptable because the expectation is that there is a certain security and assurance that marriage brings. Theoretically, someone with a spouse does not have to worry about going through life alone. The married person does not expect to be single again or go through the uncertainty of the dating process. The married person believes he or she has had some last firsts, including:

- Last first date
- Last first kiss
- Last first time meeting the family
- Last first argument
- Last first sexual encounter

The exchange of marriage vows creates a new world that eliminates things from your previous existence. The pledge—the promise to perform—must be taken seriously. A decision is only as good as the veracity of information on which it is based. For that reason alone, I hope you know what you are saying when you say "I do."

REVIEW

1. Why are people willing to sacrifice themselves to focus on their partner once they are married?

2. What does "vow" mean? What kind of promise is it?

3. What kind of expenses do we put our loved ones through when we say our vows? Why are they willing to spend so much time and money to see us at the altar?

SOUL SEARCHING

1. Why do you think people take promises so lightly these days? Do you take your promises lightly?

2. Why is it so important for the marriage vow to be meant earnestly? Consider the ideas of injury and sacrifice from this and the last chapter.

3. When you consider the amount of trust someone puts in you by believing your vow, does that influence your thoughts on keeping your promise?

SECTION

Two

The Wedding Vows: Strong Words
On That Special Day

I Take Thee

I take thee to be my wedded wife/husband; to have and to hold from this day forward, for better for worse, for richer for poorer, in sickness and in health, to love and to cherish, till death do us part, according to God's holy ordinances, I plight thee my faith.

What we know as the traditional wedding vows do not originate from the Bible. They are from the first edition of *The Book of Common Prayer*. *The Book of Common Prayer* is the book that the Church of England developed in order to give its members guides to follow, in particular the guides of sacrament and the guides of liturgy. There have been numerous editions since, but in the first edition in 1549, the ceremony didn't go quite as straightforwardly as we would think today. In fact, a couple different things could happen. Upon agreement to marry, the Church of England usually offered couples a choice. They could both promise each other to love and cherish, or alternatively, the groom could promise to love, cherish, and worship. The bride would promise to love, cherish, and obey. There were two options in the first edition. In 1922, the Episcopal Church changed it and they dropped the word obey, with the presupposition that they also would drop the word worship.

The traditional vows used in ceremonies today have different iterations. Different denominations and church orders have their own versions. Regardless of the exact verbiage, most people use some form of that original text:

I take thee to be my wedded wife/husband; to have and to hold from this day forward, for better for worse, for richer for poorer, in sickness and in health, to love and to cherish, till death do us part, according to God's holy ordinances, I plight thee my faith.

This is actually the version I use when performing weddings. For me, this version sums up the meaning and conditions of the covenant that two people enter when they get married. Except for the age-old battle centered on the word "obey," this version is true to the spirit and intent of the marriage bond. Far too often, vows are just words, especially during the wedding ceremony. Weddings at the courthouse performed by a court clerk or justice of the peace are quick and simple. Couples repeat the vows and are pronounced husband and wife.

Public wedding ceremonies are a little more involved, and they are basically about the look and the feel. The budget is mostly about the look; people spend thousands of dollars to create their preferred look. Of course, the look is important, especially to the bride and usually her mother. The wedding has to have the right dress for the bride and tuxedo for the groom. The bridal party has to be appropriately coordinated. The venue has to be well-decorated. Everything has to look good so that the pictures and video come out great. Unfortunately, spectators are prone to judge a wedding entirely on the look. They look critically at everything, from the gowns, to the flowers, even down to the hair, makeup, and shoes. Everything must look as good as the budget will allow.

The budget is about the look. The ceremony is about the feel. The wedding day is a highly emotional day for the bride and groom. The ceremony is a celebration of their relationship and family heritage, and a statement of the couple's belief system, complete with special music and tributes. When the bride and groom are finally able to stand at the altar, hand in hand, it is about the feeling. There is the wonderful, glorious feeling that they are about to be married. She is about to be his wife; he is about to be her husband. When the couple really wants to get married (that is not always the case), they stand at the altar in the middle of their own dream come true. The only things that are in the way of them becoming Mr. and Mrs. are the wedding vows and the exchange of the rings. Oh, and they can't wait to put those rings on. The rings make the statement that they are truly married. Yet, the highlight of the ceremony for the couple, the bridal party, and especially the audience, is when the bride and groom each get to say "I do" and repeat the wedding vows. Everyone is listening to hear how the bride and groom say their vows. Did their voices exude love and passion? Were they bold and strong when they said them?

Notice where the focus is. During the ceremony, the focus is on how they are saying the vows. This book focuses on *what* they are saying because, as I stated in Chapter Four, this is a decision to make a pledge. The vows are a contract. It is a pledge to live a prescribed way with your spouse and to meet predetermined responsibilities to your partner. The vows become the basic relationship requirements. The vows are a statement of what you are actually doing by getting married, and what you are assuring your partner you will do in your marriage for the rest of your life. *They are not just mere words.* Each phrase is a very powerful decision and declaration. Considering how meaningful each phrase is, let's spend the rest of the time in the book looking at the exact meaning behind the words.

I TAKE THEE

A decision has been determined. A selection has been made. "I take thee." Let's say it without the King's English. "I take you." That statement is both determinant and specific. It is a decision to choose (to "take") a particular person with whom to be in a lifetime relationship. Getting married is a decision. It is not a calling. It is not an assignment, to use church language that is presently popular. It is a decision that you make, and it is your responsibility to make it a good one. Sir, you do not get married out of obligation. Ma'am, you do not get married out of need. No one should get married out of the fear of remaining single. None of those are good reasons supporting the decision to get married. "The Lord told me," probably happens much less than people claim. To get married is a decision. I take thee. You cannot get any more direct and specific.

> To get married is a decision.

So, since your vow is a decision, when you say, "I take thee," you should know it is a good one. You should believe it with all your heart. It should not be, "I *guess* I will take you;" "I *might as well* take you;" or "I will *settle* for you." And it should definitely not be, "I'm *forced* to take you." Marriage is the greatest way to say, "I want you." Taking someone is not passive. It is a deliberate choice. I take thee. You are telling your partner, "Out of all of the other people I could have taken, I decided to take you. You were not the only option. I am not with you by chance or happenstance. You are my choice." What a great thing for a partner to know; what a great way to assure him or her. He wants her. She wants him. And the vow they make says so.

I take thee says that I do not just want to be married, I want to be married to you. It is sad but true that some people just want to be married. They are more enthralled with the thought of being married than they are in love with the one they are marrying. The partner is just a necessary part of the set. How many times have you heard women say, "My biological clock is ticking"? What about the men who have said, "Well, I guess it is time for me to settle down"?

In the '70s and '80s, I watched men get divorced and quickly get remarried. The new marriage seemingly happened in a couple of years or less. One of the reasons is because they couldn't take care of themselves. They had no domestic skills. They couldn't cook. They were not good housekeepers. They could not manage laundry, and they didn't believe they were supposed to. So, they had to get a wife. They *needed* a wife to handle domestic functions and, of course, to fulfill sexual desires. I can still hear them say to each other, "Man, I've got to get me a wife."

In the '90s, I heard women, especially single mothers, talk about marriage relative to financial considerations. The common phrase was, "I got to get me a husband. Somebody needs to help me with these bills." In many cases, they found someone they could "get along with" and got married. Even if the man wasn't very attractive to her friends, the new wife would say things like, "His check is cute."

Those relationships were about utility and necessity. People made the decision to take what someone had to offer. That is not the intent of the vows.

I take thee says to your partner, "I choose you, and you can count on that. Out of all of the other people I could have chosen or allowed to choose me, I picked you." When one person takes another in holy matrimony, they raise their romance to the status of **Most Important Interpersonal Relationship**, and their partner becomes the **Most Significant Other** in their life. The husband or wife takes the number one slot in the pecking order. I know you Christians reading this are saying that God is first, and He is. I am speaking of human relationships. When you are in a monogamous, romantic relationship, your partner has the number one slot *per se* but in a more narrow scope. Marriage puts the romantic relationship in another category.

<blockquote>
I take thee says to your partner,
"I choose you, and you can count on that…"
</blockquote>

Here is what I mean. Does the person you are dating take precedent over your parents or children, if you have them? The answer is no. Does your romantic partner take a back seat to your circle of friends? They probably should not. But, once you get married, all other relationships can only rank second and below. Your marital partner has the number one slot. The rest of your relationships do not lose their importance or significance. Everyone else in your life simply becomes lower on the pecking order.

It will be easier for some of the people in your life to understand and accept this shift than it will be for others. The keys to making this shift are communication, consistency, and care. Be caring, but communicate to your family and friends how your marriage will affect the said relationships, and be consistent in your behavior so there are no misunderstandings or mixed signals. Most will eventually adjust.

Finally, **I take thee** says that you are embracing all that comes with him or her. There is a passage of scripture that I think is extremely important when one is considering becoming a husband or wife:

The kingdom of heaven is like treasure hidden in a field. When a man found it, he hid it again, and then in his joy went and sold all he had and bought that field (Matthew 13:44, NIV84).

Although this verse is not about marriage or romantic relationships, for years, I have applied the conceptual meaning to the marital decision. A man found a treasure hidden in a field then sold all he had to buy the field. Notice that he has to purchase the field in order to take possession of the treasure. As I apply the verse, the betrothed is the treasure. No, I am not saying a person can be bought. And I am not concentrating on the fact that he sells all he has to purchase the field. That is for those who like to make the "prove how much I am worth to you" argument. That is not my thing. My focus is simple. The field accompanies the treasure. Every relationship "treasure" has a "field" that comes along with it. They are inseparable. In many cases, I have seen people who are so enamored with the treasure they have found in their relationship partner that they do not become as familiar with the field associated with the person. That is a huge mistake because it is quite possible to desire the treasure but not be able to live with the field.

It is also possible for the treasure to be great enough that your feelings about the field change. I am the head of a blended family household. My wife has two wonderful sons, with the younger of the two being nine years old at the time we got married. The funny thing is, when I began to consider the possibility of getting remarried, I made a list (much like I advised my daughter to do) of desires and a list of deal breakers concerning a potential partner. One of the deal breakers was that she could not have school-aged children living at home. I had already raised my children. They are college graduates. I had already been a middle school parent and survived. My kids had gotten out of high school pretty much unscathed and had been accepted and graduated from their university of choice. (Go Gators!) I was done. Plus, I had been a part of a blended family as a child and there are times when it does not go well. I had made up my mind that I did not ever want to have to hear the words, "You're not my daddy." Well, obviously, the deal was not broken. These days, I spend a lot of my life at little league practices and games and doing fifth grade homework. And no, I am not smarter than a fifth grader.

I did not ignore my list. I carefully and prayerfully decided to change it. After much introspection, I decided I was willing and able to accept becoming a stepfather. My wife is a treasure, and she came with a field. I made a conscious and deliberate decision to take the field accompanying the treasure. The point is, I knew the cost and decided I was willing to pay it. Many people do not act so intentionally. Some try to ignore the field. That is a mistake. Others try to change the field. Most times, that is impossible. Another deal breaker on my list was that I could not date a television or movie actress. I would not have been able to handle the love scenes. I knew that going in, so rather than frustrate a woman about her craft and chosen profession, I chose to avoid treasures with that particular field. I have had the spouses of pastors, musicians, and coaches complain about their absentee spouses. I cannot imagine what the spouse of a professional athlete goes through. But, those are the fields that came along with the treasures.

Some people try to separate the treasure from the field. It does not work long-term. The spouse will be torn trying to live a divided existence. Eventually, a choice has to be made and someone or something loses out. You have to be honest with yourself and your partner. Know what you are able and willing to handle. If you cannot handle the field, then take a pass on the treasure. It is best for both of you in the end. When you say, "I take thee," you are accepting the person and all that comes with them: their health, family dynamics, financial condition, relationship history, etc., etc., etc. Evaluate, pray, decide, and then choose. Remember, this is a treasure you're buying for life.

REVIEW

1. Where do the traditional marriage vows come from?

2. Name some of the bad reasons mentioned in this chapter for saying "I take thee."

3. How is marriage like Matthew 13:44?

SOUL SEARCHING

1. Why is it so important that the wedding vow starts with a phrase like "I take thee"? What does that imply about the relationship ahead?

2. How has the focus on the wedding ceremony taken away from the focus on the marriage? How can we correct that?

3. Did you think about the field coming along with your treasure before you got married or before your last serious relationship? What field are you bringing along into the next relationship?

My Wedded Wife, Wedded Husband

Wedded, wedding, unwed, wedlock, and newlywed are all derivations of the word "wed." To wed means to combine, fuse, or merge. To be wedded means to be bound together inseparably. These words are overwhelmingly used within the narrow context of marriage. They are not like other words that are used in various disciplines. I would guess that nine out of the ten times you hear some form of the word "wed," it involves whether or not two people have exchanged marital vows. When a couple decides to get married, they are blending themselves together into one functioning unit. Scripture puts it this way:

For this reason a man will leave his father and mother and be united to his wife, and they will become one flesh (Genesis 2:24, NIV84).

But at the beginning of creation God "made them male and female." "For this reason a man will leave his father and mother and be united to his wife, and the two will become one flesh." So they are no longer two, but one. Therefore what God has joined together, let man not separate (Mark 10:6–9, NIV84).

Every time I hear the word "inseparable," I immediately begin to hear the classic R&B ballad by the late Natalie Cole in my head.

I cannot tell you how many times I heard that song performed in junior high and high school talent shows back in my day. The song, even just its title, describes the intent of wedding. Two people are blended, fused, or merged together to become one. When two people take each other to be wedded partners they are saying to each other, "I unite myself with you. You did not cuff me. I did not cuff you. We have made a decision to combine ourselves to make one."

When we say we want to wed someone, we are using strong language and a powerful statement of our personal intent. Wedding is combining, fusing, grafting, and merging ourselves with another. Wedlock is no joke.

That is what makes divorce so heartbreaking and harmful. Divorce is not simply the undoing of a marriage; it is the opposite of marriage. To divorce is to undo, to un-blend, un-fuse, and un-merge. It is to take one flesh and make it two. It is to detach and sever what is not supposed to be. I view divorce as separating engrafted skin. How painful that must be, how lingering the injuries. It would seem impossible to detach engrafted skin without tearing a portion of skin not meant to be torn. When you try to separate what was not intended to be separated, there will be collateral damage. Divorce leaves so much collateral damage in its wake. I have firsthand knowledge. Thank God for grace, mercy, and restoration, or else those injuries would never heal at all.

The endgame of wedlock is a future secured by the presence of another whose love and care you depend on for joyous living. That is part of the assurance that comes from being married, which also means that wedlock is not meant for selfish people. If a person is selfish or self-absorbed, then they do not make their partner, nor the unit, the top priority. You do not become a wedded partner for what you can count on receiving only. Marriage is about what the other person can be assured you will give. If you are a me-first, me-only person or a me-now, you-later individual, then you are not ready for marriage. The combination of me-for-you and you-for-me is a better description of how marriage should work. Two people are blended, fused, and merged. Together. Or, as Natalie Cole would have it, "Inseparable."

MY WEDDED WHAT?

I am really big on personal capacity. I think it is paramount to understand your own personal capacity and that of those with whom you are in close relation. A person's capacity helps to determine their potential. When you have an idea of someone's capacity, you have more information to assist you in developing your expectation of who he or she is and what they can become. Have you ever heard questions like, "Is he marriage material?" or "Does she have wife potential?" Those are questions of capacity.

> When you have an idea of someone's capacity, you have more information to assist you in developing your expectation of who he or she is and what they can become.

Capacity asks the question, "Is all that I am all that I can be?" If you fill an eight-ounce glass with the same amount of liquid, you have exhausted the capacity of the glass. If you fill a 16-ounce glass with eight ounces of water, the glass has eight ounces of unused capacity. No matter how you try, you cannot make an eight-ounce glass do what a 16-ounce glass does. If you try to pour 16 ounces of water in it, you will waste eight ounces. The same is the case with people. You cannot expect to extend people beyond their capacities and expect good results.

You will read very shortly that there is a difference between a boyfriend and a husband, just like there is a difference between a girlfriend and a wife. If you date correctly, as I mentioned in Chapter Two, you can hopefully discover if someone you are dating has the capacity to grow into these bigger roles and be someone you should marry.

Not everyone can. A good dating partner or significant other may not have the capacity to meet the demands of being a husband or a wife. When you know what you expect from a wedded partner, you have to be honest with yourself and with your mate about whether your expectations can be met within that relationship. This is a very important consideration before stepping up to that altar. I have watched relationships where people live lives of unmet needs and expectations. In some cases, an individual is willing but not able. In others, a person is able but not willing. The latter is the more frustrating and usually the more difficult to accept. But, if it is the truth, it must be accepted. Better to know that before you become "wed" to that person for life.

WEDDED HUSBAND

I am a huge sports fan. My favorite sport is basketball. I follow the game very closely, watching a lot of NCAA and NBA games. I even watch the high school games that are aired on ESPN so I can see who the top college recruits are going to be. There are a few players I watched from their high school years through their professional careers. It is fun to watch who they become. It is interesting to see great college players who become average NBA players. Some do not make the league at all. On the flip side, I have seen unheralded college players become NBA stars and Hall of Famers. Why? It is because some players reach their ceiling relative to effort, talent, and attitude early, and others are not as good as they can be yet. They have unused capacity to grow, develop, and improve.

The jump from boyfriend to husband is like going from college to the NBA. No matter how good you are in the dating process, being a good husband is in another league. Trust me. I know. Some guys are immediately ready. It takes a while for others, and they cannot be judged by their rookie season. Some just don't make it. It is too much for them. Sometimes it is because, during the marriage, you find out so much more about the treasure. The field can be a bigger issue than you thought as well. A man can also get a new understanding about his own preparedness or lack thereof.

Everyone who makes a good boyfriend doesn't make a good husband. Just because he qualifies to be your "boo," doesn't mean he is qualified to be a husband. He may be great at being your man, but being a husband is next level stuff. A man should show signs that he can function on that next level before he is taken there. When man is willing to be taken as a wedded husband, he is indicating that either he has unused capacity in these areas and more, or he has the potential to build more capacity as he grows and develops.

This growth is required because the role of husband is so significant, and different, from anything a man has taken on before. A woman stands at the altar and declares, "I take you to be my wedded *husband.*" That specific word is used. She doesn't say, "I take you to be my wedded man," "my wedded baby daddy," "wedded boo," or "my wedded sweetheart." She says, "my wedded husband." The word has a very specific meaning. On the surface, it simply means male head of the household, but let's go deeper to understand the true picture. The old English etymology is so revealing. *Hus* means house. *Ban(d)* derives from a word that means holder, head, or master. In the old English, a husband was a head master or manager of a house. That is why in Aramaic, the language Jesus and his apostles spoke, husband translates as houseband as well—he who bands the house together. In John 15:1 the gardener or vinedresser is called the husbandman: *I am the true vine, and my Father is the husbandman* (KJV, 1900). The husbandman is the manager of the vineyard. He takes care of it. He is the one who weeds it, prunes it, and cleans the vines. He does everything within his power to ensure the vineyard produces a great harvest of grapes so that there can be good wine.

> This growth is required because the role of husband is so significant, and different, from anything a man has taken on before.

We have lost much of the meaning offered by the old language. A husband is a headmaster, a steward of the household. He is a leader by virtue of being a manager. When a woman says, "I take thee to be my wedded *husband*," she is making the declaration that this is the guy she can trust to lead and manage the family and household. Remember, you are not taking him as your boo. He may be good at being a boo. You're not just taking him as your best friend. He could be good at that. You're not just taking him as your lover. You are taking him as the master manager of your marital union and eventual family unit. Husband material is management material.

But, how are you to discover if he can be the headmaster of your household? How do you find out if he has the potential and promise to lead and manage? Once again, you have to be observant during the dating season. Does he manage his own affairs well? Is he an effective communicator? Is he a team player? Does he take charge without being the "boss?" Is he open to advice? Does he seek the wisdom of others? While you are taking in all the movies, enjoying the gifts, dinners, concerts, and trips to the beach, make sure you are downloading the information you need to decide if your man has the potential to be a husband.

Then, you can find out how he was raised because that can tell you a lot about him as well. Part of the dysfunction of our culture is that, too often, boys are not being raised to be responsible men. In the black community, women are raising most of the boys. The moms are doing the best they can in most cases, but as life can teach us, sometimes our best isn't good enough. Frequently, the boys are not being equipped to lead, and they get used to a woman handling their business.

I take this issue seriously, and I have the credentials to prove it. My previous book, *When I Became a Man*, is built on the premise that **males are born and men are built**. My male mentoring program is called G.A.M.E., which stands for Getting All Males Equipped. The program is so necessary because many of our boys simply are not being built and equipped to become effective heads of households.

In some of the worse cases I have seen, males are conditioned from childhood to look for women to lead and manage. Their mom or grandma has been their go-to person. If there was a problem, she solved it. If there was a decision to be made, she told them what to do. She was his nurturer, protector, provider, and caretaker. Without being given age-appropriate responsibility and intentional teaching and training on the building blocks of manhood, relationship building, and personal life management, many males do not develop what it takes to be a headmaster of a household. It is kind of sad to watch a man depend on his mother throughout his adulthood or find romantic partners who will fill the same roles with the added benefit of sensual and sexual pleasure.

Now, some women might say they don't mind if a man hasn't matured into a headmaster of a household. They want a mate who is not real husband material. The reason is, they want the power in the relationship. They want to be in total charge. I have seen women systematically choose men who are not their intellectual, spiritual, or financial equal. I have seen them employ multiple pretexts for doing so. In many cases, the real reason is they have been hurt or observed another close female be hurt. They have observed another woman give her all and have it not be reciprocated. They have watched another woman demeaned, belittled, or made to feel inferior. So, they choose relationships where they can remain the superior partner. It is a power play. It is a defensive tactic. It is an effort to reduce vulnerability. It usually ends up unsatisfying, nevertheless. A woman who decides to be a wife deep down wants a real husband. The problem is, she needs to see real husband material around, someone who deserves the title "husband."

WEDDED WIFE

The third Sunday in September is Wife Appreciation Day. Until recently, I had no idea such a day existed. I have never seen a commercial about it. I have never seen a section in the gift card aisle for it. I do not think the day is very well-known. Wives without children are to be celebrated on this day. It's a nice sentiment, but, as a matter of fact, just like a good mom, a good wife should be celebrated every day.

"I take you to be my wedded wife." That is quite a statement. "Wife" is such a powerful word. It is head and shoulders above any other term of endearment that men use. The phrase "my wife" supersedes "my girl," "girlfriend," "my lady," "my lover," or "significant other." And it definitely carries more weight than "shawty."

> "Wife" is such a powerful word. It is head and shoulders above any other term of endearment that men use.

But what is a wife? Here, unfortunately, the etymology is, at least at first glance, no help. Wife simply means "woman" in old German. Sometimes, it is easier to explain what something is by explaining what it is not. So, a wife is not just a woman. She is not just a married woman, either. She is not just a bride. That tells us that a wife is somehow more than all these things, but not what she is exactly. To be a married woman is a designation. That does not really define or describe what a wife is, especially a good one.

Turning to scripture, Genesis calls the first wife a suitable helper.

The Lord God said, "It is not good for the man to be alone. I will make a helper suitable for him" (Genesis 2:18, NIV).

New Testament scriptures speak primarily of a wife's function and how her husband should love her.

Wives, submit yourselves to your own husbands as you do to the Lord. For the husband is the head of the wife as Christ is the head of the church, his body, of which he is the Savior. Now as the church submits to Christ, so also wives should submit to their husbands in everything.

Husbands, love your wives, just as Christ loved the church and gave himself up for her to make her holy, cleansing her by the washing with water through the word (Ephesians 5:22–26, NIV).

In the same way, the women are to be worthy of respect, not malicious talkers but temperate and trustworthy in everything (1 Timothy 3:11, NIV).

I know. I know. The word "submission" and the phrase, "head of the wife" jump out at most people when they read the above verses. This book is not meant to go into the details of submission and biblical headship. I will say this: if you read the previous section on what a husband is, you can draw a couple of conclusions without even knowing how those verses read in the original language and that the English translation can be misleading in those verses. "Submission" is not synonymous with obedience, and headship does not mean the man is the chief or the boss of his wife, his suitable helper.

Maybe, just maybe, part of what scripture is trying to teach on this subject is that being a wife is a distinct function and should be a part of a woman's chosen identity. So then, a husband relates to a woman who is also his wife. Here, we do run into the original meaning of the word. The person a man marries is a woman who functions as a wife. He has to learn to love, honor, and respect both dimensions of her being. A wife is a woman, but every woman is not a wife. True womanhood is more than anatomic. There is much more in a woman to understand, engage, and appreciate.

Proverbs 31 is still the greatest picture of a wife found in scripture. As a matter of fact, the wife described in that portion of scripture is a rare super-wife.

A wife of noble character who can find? She is worth far more than rubies. Her husband has full confidence in her and lacks nothing of value. She brings him good, not harm, all the days of her life. She selects wool and flax and works with eager hands. She is like the merchant ships, bringing her food from afar. She gets up while it is still dark; she provides food for her family and portions for her servant girls. She considers a field and buys it; out of her earnings she plants a vineyard. She sets about her work vigorously; her arms are strong for her tasks. She sees that her trading is profitable, and her lamp does not go out at night. In her hand she holds the distaff and grasps the spindle with her fingers. She opens her arms to the poor and extends her hands to the needy. When it snows, she has no fear for her household; for all of them are clothed in scarlet. She makes coverings for her bed; she is clothed in fine linen and purple. Her husband is respected at the city gate, where he takes his seat among the elders of the land. She makes linen garments and sells them, and supplies the merchants with sashes. She is clothed with strength and dignity; she can laugh at the days to come. She speaks with wisdom, and faithful instruction is on her tongue. She watches over the affairs of her household and does not eat the bread of idleness. Her children arise and call her blessed; her husband also, and he praises her: "Many women do noble things, but you surpass them all." Charm is deceptive, and beauty is fleeting; but a woman who fears the LORD is to be praised. Give her the reward she has earned, and let her works bring her praise at the city gate (Proverbs 31:10-31, NIV).

Wow! What a wife she is. In summary:

- She has good character.
- Her husband trusts her judgment.

- She works hard.
- She is an industrious businesswoman with profitable business ventures.
- She is loving, caring, and benevolent.
- She plans ahead.
- She takes great care of her household.
- She is strong and dignified.
- She is a wise woman.

Proverbs 31 depicts an absolutely amazing woman and wife. You could be a really good wife and still not match her greatness. I actually think it is unfair to make her the standard. She is the dream.

To define what a wife is, I think we have to learn from all these biblical passages. A woman is trustworthy, as we see in 1 Timothy, and submissive to her family's needs, as we see in Ephesians. She is many, if not always all, of the superwoman qualities we find in Proverbs. But, I think we have to start with Genesis and conclude she is, first, God's most magnificent creation that is prepared to be an invaluable—almost irreplaceable—asset to her husband.

At the time of this writing, the presidency of Barack Obama has just ended. Regardless of your politics, you must agree that he and Michelle Obama are an amazing couple. On numerous occasions, President Obama has made clear how valuable his wife is to him. In his farewell speech, he referred to Michelle as a "girl of the south side." President Obama said, "For the past 25 years, you've been not only my wife and mother of my children, but my best friend. You took on a role you didn't ask for and made it your own with grace and grit and style and good humor.

"You made the White House a place that belongs to everybody," he continued. "And a new generation sets its sights higher because it has you as a role model. You've made me proud. You've made the country proud."

He clearly views her as his better half. My view is that it is not a matter of first and second best. In a great marriage, the two individuals within a couple are complete and whole. Each individual adds important elements to the relationship, and the two match because they function differently. They are the best thing other than Jesus to happen to each other. Hopefully, that is what leads a husband and wife to view each other as the better half of the partnership. What an incredible relationship that is, to know your individual worth but to believe that your partner adds exponential value to it.

REVIEW

1. What is the true meaning of the word "wed"?

2. What were the original meanings of the words "husband" and "wife"? How does that help us understand the roles each plays?

3. Summarize what scripture tells us about the marriage, husbands, and wives.

SOUL SEARCHING

1. Why do you think God assigned specific roles to men and women in a marriage? Do you live up to your role in your relationship or marriage?

2. Are you, or is your partner, husband material or wife material? Have you asked the right questions to be sure?

3. How can husbands and wives getting back to the basic roles outlined in this chapter help strengthen modern marriage?

Seven

To Have and to Hold
from This Day Forward

As you have probably surmised from the book so far, I think we too often overlook the meaning and intent of the traditional marriage vows. The phrases should not just be like traditional church responsive readings. Remember those? We blindly repeat what we are told. Unfortunately, that happens in wedding ceremonies. "To have and to hold from this day forward" is such a loving, romantic phrase, and yet it is often just repeated as empty sounds, a formula to get to all the romance of the ceremony.

That is a shame. The words have so much power and meaning in them if you pay attention. I have watched individuals who really understood those words say the phrase with such love and fervor, complete with dramatic pauses in some cases. When I interpret the phrase, four words come to mind: connection, attention, affection, and forever.

TO HAVE

To have a person does not speak of possession or ownership. It speaks of connection, the closest connection possible. Having a person is a matter of covenant. It says "I belong to" and not just "I belong with." This is more than affiliation or association. It is all-inclusive commitment. This commitment calls for the sharing of one's self sexually. To have requires us to act sexually, for there is no greater physical commitment. Sex is a marital privilege and a marital responsibility.

1 Corinthians 7 is a popular chapter in scripture relative to this subject. When interpreting the passage, you should understand that Paul is making a personal statement. Paul was single by choice because, to him, marriage would have gotten in the way of his ministry. He was too busy to commit to a wife. Some of you will meet people who are too busy to be married. They are too busy to be a parent. They want to be married. They want children, but they do not want marriage or parenthood to interfere with their schedules. Everybody in their life is trying to fit into what they already have going on. Paul says, "I'm not going to do that to a woman. I got to go. So, since I know I have to go, I'm not going to have a wife." He chooses not to have a wife. He says it is good not to marry, but, since there is such potential for immorality, each man should have his own wife and each woman her own husband.

Here is Paul's understanding: he says, "I wish everybody was single because single people are more free to do God's work." It is the single people who should be doing the most work in church because you do not have the responsibility of marriage. If you are a wife or husband, you can't be at church every time the door opens. You have a responsibility to your spouse and to your relationship. If Valentine's Day falls on "church night," I think it is ridiculous to require married people to be present. Many churches and pastors do not agree. We lay a heavy guilt trip on the absent couples by saying the Lord comes first. This is unfair. When you nurture your marital relationship, it is a statement of your commitment to God. I have seen the irresponsible commitment to ministry and church activities destroy marriages, especially those of pastors and ministers. Some end in divorce. Others continue on in misery. That is more displeasing to God than a missed church night or two.

> When you nurture your marital relationship, it is a statement of your commitment to God.

The responsibility of taking care of the marital relationship comes through clearly in Paul's epistle. This includes a responsibility to put other things aside (yes, sometimes even church), in order to take care of your spouse. It also has other implications. In 1 Corinthians 7:3, Paul says, *"The husband should fulfill his marital duty to his wife and likewise the wife to her husband"* (NIV). It gets deeper. Verse 4: The wife's body does not belong to her alone but also to her husband in the same way the husband's body does not belong to him alone but also his wife. So, when you get married, if there is a signature on your body of ownership, you've got to add another line, because you are no longer a single owner. There is now a co-owner. It is your spouse. That is one of the reasons adultery is so bad. You are taking something that belongs to somebody else and giving it away. In marriage, you and your spouse are co-owners of each other's body.

Now, let's talk about agreement and what this does not say. It does not say that in any situation that you ought to be able to get sex on demand. There is a presupposition of agreement. There is a presupposition of understanding and even the laws on the books now say you can prove rape from a spouse. No means no, even if it is your spouse.

Here is what Paul, and the wedding vow, mean. As one author puts it, the Bible says that the spouses own each other's body for the purpose of sexual activity, but that does not mean it gives license to act unlovingly in the process. Offering your body and your affection willingly while also considering what the spouse wants is what I believe the vow means.

Agreement from both partners is so important because sex is supposed to include the body, mind, and the emotions. Sex is not just a physical exchange; it is also a blending of the souls. The Bible says, *"and the two will become one flesh"* (Mark 10:8, NIV). When people have sex, two bodies become one with each other. But, because sex is not just a physical connection but an emotional one as well, sex, then, is an act of the soul as well as the body. If a person is emotionless during sex, then it is merely recreational. Physical gratification is achieved without any other exchange. If a person cannot exchange emotions with you during that process, it is purely recreational.

Recreational sex is a depreciated form of sex as given to us by God. It cheapens it and places it in the category of sport like pick-up basketball, tennis, or golf. We get personal pleasure out of sports, and of course, there are health benefits to keeping active. The more you play, the better you get. The better you get the more you look for players of similar and more advanced skills to play with. Who the people are is inconsequential. You are not trying to know them on a deeper level. It is your common love for the game and your ability and availability to play that matters. So it is when sex is recreational. We engage in it out of physical need and desire and find a favorite partner to play. The sacred act of sex is now simply physical, hormonal, and in some cases, therapeutic.

Unfortunately, premarital sex is the norm in this country. Whether it is between people who really love and care for each other or the "I don't want to sleep alone tonight" kind, it has become the expected thing to do. As a matter of fact, in today's culture, we ridicule and even shame unmarried virgins. Sex is used to sell everything from toothpaste to cheeseburgers. Popular music is sexually charged and social media allows us to keep up with the bed partners of celebrities.

Here is a quick sidebar for the single ladies. Single women need to realize that some men will go to great lengths once they decide they want to be sexually involved with a particular woman. He will tell you whatever he has to tell you and buy you whatever he has to buy you. He will be loving, thoughtful, and considerate in ways he may not be able to continue. That type of man will do whatever it takes to make it happen once he decides he wants a sexual experience with you. So, you have to be very careful not to fall for that. He will even tell you he loves you. Sometimes, it is totally disingenuous. Other times, he's really caught up in the pursuit, and he actually thinks the actions are natural and the words are true. Unfortunately, the truth is not discovered until after there is sexual involvement. Both the man and the woman then discover what is real and what is not about their courtship.

Well, what about when the love *is* real, you might say? I still encourage couples to leave sex out because it can affect relationship development. The moral and spiritual implications are known and have been discussed in this book to some degree already. In addition to all that, premarital sexual activity can also damage the natural progression of growth and maturity in a relationship. Sex can change the focus of a relationship, create false positive energy, and mask problems that need to be uncovered and solved.

Once a dating couple starts having sex, everything else in the relationship can be affected. Sex can become the central and most viable part of a union. Sex can be just that powerful. It can shift focus and motives. You no longer talk just to be talking. You're talking about the last time you had sex and when you are going to have it again. You no longer go out to dinner just to hang out. You take her out to dinner so you can have sex after. You go to the movies so you can have sex. We have all heard of the "Netflix and chill" phenomenon, in which Netflix is just an excuse for another sexual encounter. You buy her a gift, and the nicer the gift, the sooner the sex. Everything starts to be built around sex.

What is even scarier is that relationships can be built *on* sex. Sex can create false energy. A relationship can be on fire because of bad fuel. Two people can get that caught up in sex. Your emotional, psychological, and physical connection for a person can really get you "twisted" as we used to say. I know for some people, sharing their body is the greatest expression of love, but if you are not careful, sharing your body can make you feel like you are in love. I have often coached people with this bit of wisdom. If someone tells you they love you for the first time either immediately before, during, or right after sex, you may want to be careful about how much faith you put in their words. I'm just saying. I say it because sexual involvement can energize the relationship and make everything else seem better, even if in actuality it is not good.

Perhaps that all sounds alright to you, but there are real costs to letting sex take over a relationship. When sex narrows the focus of a relationship, the other aspects are hidden or avoided. People get married and discover they have very little in common. She isn't interested in the things he is. He does not like her worldview, her mentality, or her general disposition. He is not an open communicator. She has severe daddy issues. All of that was hidden or ignored because of the positive energy of a good sexual connection. The relationship had a false positive. Now, those people are contemplating a painful, injury-causing divorce, perhaps with kids also involved.

Or, perhaps that couple just tries to hide their dysfunction behind more sex. If you are not careful, sex can mask conflict. It can become the go-to conflict resolution agent. It can be the one thing that a couple has that keeps them together. Again, short-term, this can feel like a good solution. Make-up sex can keep you problem-free for a period of time. However, the problem, sooner or later, will surface again if it is not properly addressed, and it will have grown to be much worse. I have seen people maintain dysfunctional, damaging relationships because their chemistry always gave them hope that things could work out. Sometimes it does. Most times it does not. The results when it does not are particularly bad.

Many church people are probably saying that I have spent an inordinate amount of time on the subject of premarital sex. Well, saints of the most high God, you charter and neophyte members of the religious elite, this may be a good time to dismount your high horse. Single people are extremely sexually active even in the church. Research says that 80 percent of Christians engage in premarital sex. Not the world. *Christians.* Tongue-talking, hand-waving, toe-tapping *Christians.*

What is interesting in church is the duplicity regarding this subject. We really only confront or condemn people if they are adulterers or if the sexual relationship produces a child. Rarely is something said about premarital sexual activity among single adults who practice "safe" sex. As a church, we really need to clean up our act when it comes to this. We condemn and place a scarlet letter on people if they have a baby out of wedlock or sleep with someone who is married. Somehow, we rarely confront those we know are unmarried and sexually active. We need to be more consistent. Scripture speaks about the act as sin. The Bible does not limit itself to the repercussions we deem wrong or immoral.

The standards of our culture progressively change. Even a child out of wedlock is not viewed the way it once was. I guess it is now considered a victimless sin. Adultery, on the other hand, still has a victim, the spouse, who has been cheated on. That doesn't mean other forms of premarital sex are okay, though. Adultery breaks covenant with God and another individual, but fornicating still breaks covenant with God and a person's own body. Sin is sin; the consequences are just different.

Here is what is spiritually and relationally optimal. Two well-adjusted virgins date appropriately, develop love, and get married. They stay married until death without ever having sex with anyone else. They "have" and they "hold" only each other. Trust me, I know how boring that sounds to many of you. As I am writing, I can mentally picture people I know who are turning up their noses. Yet, it is optimal for several reasons. First, it pleases God. Second, each partner has no emotional and spiritual residue from sexual encounters with other people (and therefore can give their entire soul to that one spiritual and sexual commitment). Third, there are no comparisons to be made with another person.

Those are pretty strong reasons, as even those turning up their noses have to admit, which underscores an important lesson that

I've learned about God. When He tells us not to do something, He is not just depriving us. He is telling us for our own good because he knows what can negatively affect us down the road. When we disobey Him, there is always a price to pay. That's why, when we get married and have a sexual history, we should ask the Holy Spirit to cleanse our heart, mind, soul, and spirit of the residue of previous sexual encounters so that it does not affect our present relationship. That's why it's a shame we have to ask to be cleansed in the first place.

> When we disobey Him, there is always a price to pay.

In the end, God gave us sex to enjoy within the confines of marriage. He created it for us. He gave it to us. He created it so we could "have" one another and "hold" one another, and so that two people could become one. Thank you, Jesus.

Within the bounds of marriage, you can even ask God to help you. What? Yes, you can. You can pray and ask God to help you and your spouse to have a fulfilling, enjoyable physical relationship.

Sex is not dirty. It is not evil. It is holy within the context of marriage, and whatever God has given me to enjoy I can take to Him in prayer. So, if you are in a marriage where part of the problem is sexual incompatibility, discuss it and pray about it. Get help from a qualified Christian therapist, if necessary. If you are engaged, make sure you discuss your thoughts, feelings, and expectations with your future spouse. Don't be coy, and don't be misleading or dishonest.

Sex is very important to your marriage. That's why it's alluded to in the vows. It's part of what we're promising our spouse at the altar, part of what God promised us when He created us. It's a wonderful part of a romantic relationship, but the vow has to come first.

TO HOLD

I dare say, there is not a person alive who at some point did not or does not want to be held. When someone is held, they feel loved and assured. Holding someone can soothe their pain or stop their panic. It is a reminder that they are not alone. Sometimes, it says "I love you" better than the actual words.

When the one you love wraps his or her arms around you, pulls you close, and keeps you there, it causes a warm feeling. When physical contact is your "love language"—one of the five ways a person, by default, shows love, according to author Gary Chapman, who wrote *The Five Love Languages*—you especially love being held. This is more than just hugging. A good hug is one thing, but being held is exponentially better. Being held is more intensely intimate, more unmistakably loving and protective. I have had plenty of bad hugs. I have given my share of them as well. I have received some unwanted hugs. I have given a few as well. How do I know? People's body language can immediately let you know whether or not they want you to hug them. That's not the case with being held. Under normal circumstances, no one holds anyone or gets held against their will. Holding someone is an intentional act and being held is volitional. "Please hold me" is a very personal and intimate request. It suggests trust and a need for comfort. A person is willingly putting themselves in a vulnerable position. That's why the one being asked makes the effort and initiates the embrace. The one being held receives the gesture, and they both enjoy the sustained embrace. It is a genuine physical act of love and protection. It is a win-win.

So, on their wedding day, two people promise to hold each other for the rest of their lives. What does that mean? Does that mean to physically hold them, to hold on to them, or, as we say in urban America, to hold them down? I believe it means all of the above. When you vow to have and to hold your spouse, it means you agree to give them the love and care that she or he will need over the course of a lifetime. You owe it to them because you promise you will provide it when you stand at the altar. "To have" your spouse is the benefit of the marital covenant that draws you closer and makes you one. "To hold" your partner is your promise to intentionally nurture and preserve the relationship by giving him or her the affection and attention they require. When you say, "I want to have you, and I want to hold you," you are saying that you want to actively care for your spouse in every physical, emotional, and spiritual sense.

Your vows tell you that your goals should be to be your partner's chief supporter, number one fan, and ride-or-die partner. You work to make every burden lighter and every day brighter. You protect your mate's well-being while making daily substantial contributions to their happiness. When you hold your spouse, you do the things necessary for the relationship to be solid and fulfilling for both of you. "To have" can be a selfish act. If we are not careful, we can make sex primarily or solely about our individual need. "To hold," on the other hand, is totally unselfish and requires trust that your partner is acting the same way. When you commit to hold your mate, in essence, you say to them, "I got you. No matter what, I got you." Now, that is marriage for real.

How well do you have to know your companion to make that vow? How well should you know yourself and your capacity before making such a commitment? I think the answer is, "extremely well," on both accounts. You should know yourself well enough to have a handle on your own needs and expectations, and you should know your spouse well enough to be clear on theirs.

It should be understood that your partner's needs and expectations may be different than yours. One of the reasons relationships fail is that we manage our relationships as if the needs of both genders are identical. When we operate under that false premise, we give our partners what would be satisfactory to us. Then, we wonder why they are not content with the relationship.

William Harley wrote a book entitled *His Needs, Her Needs* (2011). I recommend it to all the couples I coach. The premise of the book is that the needs of a woman are different than the needs of a man. Men and women are different, and they have particular needs. Their needs are not identical and in some cases not even similar. For instance, men need sex while women need affection. Sex and affection are cousins and not twins. Men require recreational companionship and domestic support while most women demand conversation and financial support. I tend to believe that these needs are not mutually exclusive and can be a desire or necessity for both genders. It is simply an issue of the level or intensity of the need.

Harley makes generalizations to make his point. In your relationship and marriage, you need to know the specifics regarding your partner's needs. In my premarital coaching, I share that those needs should be known, communicated, and agreed upon.

In order to do this effectively, individuals should separate nonnegotiable needs from negotiable desires. What are your four or five basic, absolute needs in a relationship? This list is the same no matter who the partner is. I have to know myself well enough to know what is to be on that list. A person who does not know what they need should not be thinking of marriage.

Once I know what my needs are, it is my responsibility to effectively communicate them to my partner. If she agrees that she has the capacity, will, and desire to meet those needs, then we have an agreement. I cannot stress enough that your partner should have knowledge of your nonnegotiable needs along with the capacity, desire, and will to meet them. If you have capacity without will and desire, you will leave your partner wanting. Will and desire without the capability is a complete fail. Both parties will be exasperated.

Sir, you really do want to please your wife, right? It is a given that you want to do everything you can to contribute to your wife's happiness, isn't it? Sis, you want to be a primary contributor to you husband's happiness, don't you? The correct answer is "yes." This sentiment is usually automatic at the onset of the marriage. In the beginning, we are usually very focused on pleasing our mate. We want to see them happy. We love putting a smile on the face of our loved one. We are energized by their joy. As the variables of life increase, our focus can become divided and effort no longer accompanies sentiment. Career pursuits, children, and even church activities can shift attention away from our spouse, if we allow it. There are only 24 hours in each day, and we all have a limited amount of physical, mental, and emotional energy to use in accomplishing our daily agendas. If we are not careful, we can forget, or simply fail to save, the time and energy needed to attend to our mate.

Before you know it, you are committing one of the cardinal sins of marriage: neglect. Neglect will kill your marriage, and it can be a slow, painful death. Death by neglect does not always end in divorce. Two people can remain together even when their marriage is graveyard dead. Once again, I reference Harley. The subtitle of *His Needs, Her Needs* is "Building an Affair-Proof Marriage." I am sure that got your attention. I am glad he uses the word "build." Good marriages do not just happen. Strong marriages are not a matter of chance. Couples must do the necessary work for their marriages to flourish and be fortified.

Harley says that every one of us has an emotional bank account, and we make daily deposits and withdrawals in our partner's account. Your goal should be to make more deposits than withdrawals and for those deposits to be of greater value than the withdrawals. Your account with your partner should always have a positive balance. In your relationship, you always want to operate in the black.

The accounting here is relatively simple. When you add value to your partner, by assisting them or complimenting them or supporting them, you are making a deposit. A big hug at the perfect time or a "just because" gift is a huge deposit. When you make a demand on the relationship or fail to meet needs and expectations, you are making a withdrawal. Conflict can be a withdrawal. Proper conflict resolution, though, can be a deposit. The key, regardless of the specifics, is to make sure your deposits are more substantial than your withdrawals so that you maintain a positive account balance.

We always have to keep an eye on our balance because when the emotional currency is gone, it's gone. I remember when my son, Donovan, was a toddler. He didn't understand how money and banking worked. He asked me to buy him something, and I told him that I did not have any money. His reply was, "Go to the ATM." That was a reasonable solution to him. He thought money came out of the

ATM automatically. At that age, he did not know that, in order to get money out of the bank, you had to have some in it. He did not know that, on that particular day, we had no extra money to withdraw from the bank.

Have you ever had your debit card denied? I know people do not write many checks anymore, but have you ever had a check bounce? In both cases, the account holder tried to make a withdrawal that could not be processed because of a low balance. More withdrawals had been made than deposits.

So, have you checked your marital account lately? Have you been making more deposits than withdrawals? What is your balance? The emotional account activity is happening at all times whether it is intentional or unintentional. If you are making the requisite deposits to cover your withdrawals, then you are okay. If not, then one day, your check is going to bounce or your card is going to be denied. There will be insufficient emotional funds. Your spouse will not be there for you when you need them. What you depend on from them will no longer be accessible.

I mentioned earlier that the subtitle of Harley's book is "Building an Affair-Proof Marriage." That proposition is tied to his theory about the emotional bank. He says we will be most connected to the people who make the most deposits. In light of this, it is important that no person of the opposite sex makes more deposits in your partner's account than you. If that is not the case, you risk your spouse and that person developing an emotional connection that can become greater than the one your companion has with you.

Sir, if you never have time to converse, but a coworker always shares and listens, then his account balance is rising. Sis, if you are not interested in anything he does, but his old classmate is encouraging and supportive, then her account balance is getting higher. Research suggests that, for many people, adultery is not about sex but about unmet needs. Now, some people commit adultery because they enjoy the excitement of sexual variety. But, frequently, adultery is part of a progression that begins when a spouse and someone outside the marriage develop a substantial level of emotional intimacy. Attachment morphs into attraction. Affinity and familiarity evolve into romantic feelings. Unbridled romantic feelings lead to sinful, adulterous sex that in turn devastates and potentially destroys a marriage. This is not meant to be an excuse and definitely not a justification, but the reality is, there is usually a motivation behind affairs, and you can keep that motivation out of your household if you know the right accounting tricks.

Which brings us back to "holding." Let me repeat a couple of earlier statements:

- To hold your partner is your promise to intentionally nurture and preserve the relationship by giving him or her the affection and attention they require.
- When you vow "to have and to hold" your spouse, it means you agree to give them the love and care that she or he will need over the course of a lifetime.

That is a major commitment, but it is the key to keeping a marriage together and alive and well.

FROM THIS DAY FORWARD

The traditional wedding vows emphasize that marriage is meant to be for life. Within the vows are two references to marriage as a lifetime commitment. The phrase "till death do us part" is commonly known. In some iterations, it is replaced with "as long as we both shall live." Either way, the point is made. The second reference is in the words that follow "to have and to hold": "from this day forward." Again, the point is made: marriage is meant to be for life. To have and to hold from this day forward says, "I know who I want to accompany me as I walk into an unknown future." It is a commitment to embrace each other as you face each day together. Church people, I know you have Jesus and the Holy Spirit, but having a ride-or-die partner in your husband or wife is an added blessing. Having a spouse is knowing who is going to be in your bed and in your corner for the rest of his or her life. That is the intent. Unfortunately, in the United States, it doesn't happen 50 percent of the time. The average length of a marriage that ends in divorce is eight years. What is supposed to be forever usually does not even last a decade.

> To have and to hold from this day forward
> says, "I know who I want to accompany me
> as I walk into an unknown future."

"Forever" is such a nice, romantic word. It is really cute to hear lovebirds proclaim that they want to be together forever and ever and ever. My definition of forever is not so romantic, but it is reality. Forever is every day until you die. So, at a wedding, two people stand and declare they will make a daily commitment to each other until one of them takes a final breath. That may sound extreme in the world we live in, but that is the gig. Marriage is a fresh commitment made to your spouse every day until you die. I know. I know. That is not romantic, but it is real talk. If you like the word "forever" better, then use it, but do not forget what I told you. Forever is every day until you die. Hey, lovebirds, you can handle that, can't you?

One of my favorite questions to ask during my premarital coaching sessions is, "If the person you desire to marry never changes for the rest of your lives, are you okay with that?" I further elaborate, "If your partner never improves, never comes around, or never makes the shift, will that work for you? Is who they presently are satisfactory to you for the rest of your life? If the answer is 'no,' you probably should not get married."

Those questions are intended to be a dose of reality. Many people unconsciously make a lifetime commitment to the person they hope their partner will become. They have the idea that certain things will change over time or under the right circumstances. But, at the altar, you exchange vows with who the person is, not who you hope they become.

In Chapter Two, we discussed the importance of capacity and future growth in the context of dating well. This is not a contradiction but a different frame of reference. Potential and future capacity can be detected. When you know it is there, couples can grow together. Here, I am warning you against making a vow you know you cannot keep. The marital commitment is to have and to hold from the wedding day forward. That is a lifetime. That is forever. A groom does not say, "To have and to hold contingent upon if she changes her bad attitude." The bride does not say, "To have and to hold unless he doesn't learn to hold a steady job and manage money better." It is, "From this day forward." If the person you marry has known deal breakers in their character or behavior, if you can't accept the field that comes with the treasure from that day forward, then you are making a vow you probably cannot keep for a lifetime. Forever is a very long time, and making a lifetime commitment to have and hold that one person should be a prayerful, calculated decision.

REVIEW

1. What does "to have" mean in the marriage vows? What about "to hold"? How are these qualities important to marriage?

2. What are some of the negative consequences of having sex outside of the marriage covenant?

3. How can sex enrich a marriage?

4. Why do we need to make sure we deposit more into our marriage account than we withdraw?

5. Why do we need to be comfortable with the person we marry from day one? Consider the vow "from this day forward."

SOUL SEARCHING

1. Think back over your previous sexual experiences. How would they have been enriched if they were shared with only one person?

2. If you are still a virgin, what has allowed you to maintain your purity in the face of so much social pressure? If not, what would you tell a virgin to help them in that situation?

3. How can we begin to change society's obsession with premarital sex?

4. Have you kept your marriage account balance at a healthy level? What can you do to start making more deposits?

5. How can you both look for a partner with room to grow and be comfortable with who they are from day one?

Eight

For Better for Worse.
For Richer for Poorer.
In Sickness and in Health.

Since 1995, ESPN has held the X Games annually. Extreme sports are very popular around the world. They are dangerous and exciting, or maybe they are exciting because they are dangerous. Extreme sport athletes are talented, skilled, and daring. I mean, you have to be brave to do base-jumping, snowboarding, skateboarding, or wing-suit diving as a sport. Extreme sports involve either height or speed, and sometimes both. These athletes have my highest respect, although I have no interest in participating in any of their sports.

I like being on the ground, unless I am in an airplane. I do not really care for heights. There will be no cliff diving or bungee jumping for me. I have a pretty fast car. It satisfies any need I have for speed. I do not even like rollercoasters. I just do not have the stomach for them. Virtual reality games and rides give me motion sickness as well. At amusement parks, I was the person watching the bags while my family rode the daring rides. Eventually, I stopped going at all and just paid for my kids to go. I learned through trial and error that most amusement park rides are not for me. My stomach just cannot handle the extreme changes in speed and motion. After getting ill several times and losing my lunch on one occasion, I learned my limits. I cannot fathom participating in an extreme sport. Whenever I happen to watch the X Games, the athletes seem to be intensely competitive while having a lot of fun. My thoughts are that I would never, ever do that stuff. It is just not safe.

In a sense, marriage is also unsafe. I know I have mentioned that having a spouse brings a level of security and assurance, and that is true. Yet, this section of the traditional vows reminds us that there are parts of marriage that are a little unsettling, a little extreme, and, humanly speaking, a little unsafe.

Let me say, right off the bat, that this is the section of the vows that many, if not most, brides and grooms really do not mean. "I take you for better or worse, for richer or poorer, in sickness and in health." That is the X Games of promises, the language of extremes. Common threads among the different X Games events are speed, severe highs and lows, and the possibility that someone could always get hurt. The nature of marriage is very similar in that way. While I hope speed is not a factor, there are definitely highs and lows, and people can be hurt. With the exception of the final phrase, in sickness and in health, this section is often viewed as conceptual or metaphorical and not necessarily literal. But the vows are the vows. The delineation is simple and clear: For better for worse, for richer for poorer, in sickness and in health.

Those statements are conceptual but in a very concrete way. The statements are examples of the extremes, both the fun and exciting extremes and the dangerous ones. They are polar opposites. The message is this: brides and grooms promise to stay committed to one another in the extremes of life and everything in between.

That is a logical extension from where the vows last left us. Although this book explains the vows in sections, we should remember that they are intended to be taken as a whole. The vows seem like a setup if not taken as a complete unit. Let me explain. The promise is made "to have and to hold" from this day forward, *then* the context is added. As I said before, the treasure comes with the field. The field is full of extremes and everything in-between. The beauty of the marriage vows is they make serious reality sound gloriously romantic. And I agree, there is something romantic in a marriage that is stable, powerful, and beautiful, one where the couple can sustain romance while daily embracing reality. But, marriage is more than your promise to engage and enjoy life with your mate. When necessary, it is also a promise to endure it. You commit to the mountains, the valleys, and the range of varied experiences. You are on board for the highs and the lows, for the breakneck speeds and the Sunday afternoon strolls. When you repeat the marriage vows, you tell another individual, "On my best day, I want you. On my worst day, I still want you. In the penthouse or the projects, on Everest or stuck in a ditch, I want you."

> The beauty of the marriage vows is they make
> serious reality sound gloriously romantic.

Let me say again. The poetic nature of the vows makes serious reality sound romantic. It is easy to get caught up in the emotions provoked by the words. But the words matter. The words have to become incarnated into the life of the marriage. The vows, in part, set the parameters of the relationship. They clearly articulate that, in marriage, a couple commits to a full range of experiences, even if many only prepare themselves subconsciously for the middle ground and the positive extremes.

Of course, I have coached and advised couples in conflict. It can be painful to be locked in an office with two people who are presently unhappily married. On several occasions, I have heard a husband or a wife make statements such as, "This is not what I expected," or "I didn't sign up for this." Pain can cloud our memory, but unfortunately, many of us just weren't paying attention and were just repeating words when we said our vows. When we said the words, we committed to a wide range of experiences. We signed up for the peaks and valleys, but subconsciously, we only prepared ourselves to enjoy the positive extremes and not to embrace and endure the negative ones. Sure, we had in mind there would be problems and difficulties, but not extreme situations. But, uh, that's what we said. It may not have been what we meant, but it is what we said. And the words matter.

Does the thought of the unknown possibilities of marriage make anyone other than me think of how important the God factor is right now? Please allow me this one preachy moment. If you commit to the extremes of marriage, you want to be sure that the presence, power, and providence of God are active in your life and in the relationship. You want to be sure He is in favor of the relationship so that it has His blessing upon it. The God factor is critical to the success of the relationship and to the constancy of individual peace and security because He is the one who knows the future and has power over it. His presence, power, and providence assure you that it is possible to handle whatever lies ahead in your relationship. The eternal God will provide for you and sustain the relationship, as you and your partner engage in whatever extremes life throws at you.

Don't expect God to do all the lifting, though, even if He blesses your marriage. I have learned that God will not do for us what we can do for ourselves.

The best way to bring God into a marriage and avoid some of the worst extremes in marriage is to make sure you've chosen the right person to say the vows to in the first place. As was discussed in Chapter Two, there is no substitute for effective dating. Dating is a discovery period, which is why, generally speaking, couples should date for a while before getting married. Some things are discovered over time. Short-term relationships can be misleading because everything is so great the first few months. I mean, if they weren't, why bother, right? "We don't argue. I like everything he likes. He likes everything I like. He's funny and polite. He loves God." Ok, Carol Brady, how long have you and Mike been together? "Two months." Man! Aren't new relationships just grand?

It's wonderful to feel all that excitement and that rush of happiness, but how do you know yet if your relationship can handle **for better for worse**? Have you dated in a way to discover whether your partner can handle the extremes? How is your mate when on the mountain? How is he or she in the valley? People can change depending on the circumstances. It is important to have an idea of the full scope of your mate's beliefs, tendencies, behavioral patterns, and attitude. You should learn those things while you are dating. If you date long enough, there will be highs and lows in the relationship, and *life* will happen to one or both of you. Character is revealed by both success and stress. Who is he when things are going phenomenally well? Does he remain focused on the relationship even when he is riding high? Is it important to him for you to share in his success or does he become dismissive or inattentive? Some people are intolerable when they are on top of the world. Who is she when under stress? How does your partner handle conflict? Are they repentant when they offend? Are they forgiving when hurt or offended? What are they like when they are angry? Dr. Bruce Banner was a mild-mannered scientist, but when he got angry, he became the Incredible Hulk. You need to know all you can and have an idea about the rest so that you can forecast as accurately as possible.

And, perhaps the most important question you can ask while dating is: What are your partner's levels of faith and spirituality? True faith and spiritual maturity are revealed during hardship and difficulty. You learn a lot about a person when you see them go through a test or trial or while you are going through one and need their support. Does he or she have any real faith? Can you believe in God together? Will you fight the enemy as a unit? Can you count on each other's prayers? When a difficult trial comes, you do not want to be the only one in the relationship with real faith. You should be able to have confidence in your mate's ability to think spiritually and act in faith. What if, in a time of personal weakness, you need to lean on your partner's spirituality?

> True faith and spiritual maturity are revealed during hardship and difficulty.

That need can come to any of us, even those most invested in God and faith. Don't believe me? Just look at Moses. I love the story of Moses. It is one of my favorite personal narratives in scripture. Moses, the great prophet, led the children of Israel out of Egypt and across the Red Sea, but it would have never happened without his wife, Zipporah.

FOR BETTER FOR WORSE. FOR RICHER FOR POORER.
IN SICKNESS AND IN HEALTH.

On the way to Egypt, at a place where Moses and his family had stopped for the night, the Lord confronted him and was about to kill him. But Moses' wife, Zipporah, took a flint knife and circumcised her son. She touched his [Moses'] feet with the foreskin and said, "Now you are a bridegroom of blood to me." (When she said "a bridegroom of blood," she was referring to the circumcision.) After that, the Lord left him alone (Exodus 4:24–26, NLT).

That's right! Zipporah fought for her husband's life, ministry, and destiny. Moses had frustrated God with his lack of faith. She knew what could save him and got it done. She took action to fight for her husband to have another chance to pursue his purpose. She interceded for Moses when he was in trouble with God. Moses was alive and in place to lead the children of Israel out of Egypt because of his strong, spiritual wife. I love that sister!

FOR BETTER FOR WORSE

Zipporah was there for Moses at his lowest, at the extreme of their marriage. That is what the vows call on all of us to do. She definitely made it through the "worse" end of her marriage. She understood what she was committing to when she agreed to marry, and we are all the better for it.

The traditional vows highlight categories of polar opposite extremes in order to prepare all of us for our Zipporah-Moses moment. Following logically one upon another, they move from the general to specific. It starts with the phrase "for better or for worse," which is universal and all encompassing. Better what? Worse what? Better how? Worse how? Better when? Worse when? Your life will answer all of those questions. Time will fill in the blanks. When you say you will spend the rest of your life with someone, you commit to embrace years of the unknown with them. Life is an adventure, and what a blessing it is to have someone to take the ride with you. But, the future is nevertheless unknown and will hold some good days and bad days. The marriage vow is a commitment to both extremes, the best and the worst. Imagine the best time possible for you and your partner where you would be able to say, "It just doesn't get any better than this." Come on, envisage the best time ever. Are you on a dream vacation or purchasing your dream house? Is it the birth of a child? Is it the thought of being loved, honored, accepted, and appreciated on a daily basis for the rest of your life? Well, all of that is marriage.

I wish there was not a flip side, but there is. You and your spouse will experience challenges during your marriage. That is a guarantee. You can bank on it. The great thing about it is you will not have to face those negative circumstances on your own. When tough times come, you will not be alone. You will have someone to share your problems and to partner with you as you endure your pain.

But, that doesn't mean there won't be pain. The most difficult pain to manage is that which is caused by your partner, directly or indirectly. It can be agonizing when your relationship is not going well. When your partner hurts you, the pain can be intense. The fact that you live with them makes it worse. Sometimes, physical distance helps the healing process. You do not get any with your spouse, so unfortunately, people create emotional distance which is detrimental to the relationship. But, you have to find a way through it. That's what you promised. No matter how bad it can get, you are going to work through it. That's the "worse." You've got to work back to the "better" together.

When two people are dating, it is abnormal to wonder about how tough things could become. An engaged couple is not worried about relationship trouble while they are planning their wedding. Yet, the vows are there to warn the loving, happy couple that the road can get rough and the going can get tough. How bad can an experience be? How long can the bad times last before they get better? I do not have an answer to those questions. I do suggest that the individuals within the couple learn to forgive and be forgiven and to reconcile quickly, as scripture teaches. I also recommend that you incorporate friendship as well as *agape* love within your relationship. Romantic love is not sufficient to sustain a marriage. *Eros* performs well during "for better," but not so much in the middle of "for worse." And lastly, do not hesitate to get outside help. A seasoned couple, a wise pastor, or a certified marriage and family therapist could be just what you need to protect your marriage from what should be temporary difficulty. Do the work you promised to do so love and marriage can last.

Think about it like this. If someone said you were going to be married for 50 years and 47 of them would be happy, you would take that would you not? Compare 47 good years to three bad ones. It does not compare, does it? We must try to remember that trouble does not last forever while we are going through a tough time. There is far more "better" around the corner once we get through that rough patch of "worse."

FOR RICHER FOR POORER

Trading Places, starring Eddie Murphy and Dan Aykroyd, is one of my favorite movies. The movie's storyline is that a poor and destitute man abruptly trades places with a man who is wealthy and privileged. Overnight, a poor man is rich, and a rich man finds himself broke and homeless. Each character is totally immersed in the other's lifestyle and has to immediately learn to function.

Trading Places is a comedy. It is funny to see how a homeless Eddie Murphy learns to live in a mansion with servants and a chauffeur and work on Wall Street, while a filthy rich Dan Aykroyd learns to make it on the streets. The lifestyle of the rich is drastically different from that of the poor, and that lends itself to some very funny situations when done well. In reality, we know that rich versus poor is no laughing matter. Rich is the polar opposite of poor. The contrast is extreme.

When you say this portion of the marital vows, you move from the very general to something a little more concrete: you commit to whatever your fiscal future becomes during your marriage. Husbands and wives are business partners working together for the financial success of the family. Repeating the vows is an acknowledgement that, together, you are willing to live with any of the potential economic peaks and valleys that transpire within your relationship. This is a critical assertion because, according to several sources, money is the number one reason for marital conflict. Our connection to money and what it does for us is emotional. I would venture to say it is spiritual. Scripture says that the love of money is the root of all evil. It may well provide many great advantages in life, but we have to keep that warning fresh in our minds.

The attachment to money can be extremely strong, which is why scripture also warns us not to serve mammon. People can be so attached to their money that they remain in loveless, miserable relationships in order not to lose any of it.

Basically, good or bad, a lot or a little, money matters. Sure, marriage is about the love two people have for each other, but it also pertains to the life that two people can build together. Most people have an expectation of the lifestyle they desire to live. Most of us have mental pictures of our dream existence. In reality, we anticipate living somewhere between our basic expectations and our dream life. Of course, we Christians know that God is able to do exceedingly above all we could ask or imagine. The fact still remains, we fancy a certain style of living and have financial goals we want to meet. When those goals and expectations are not met, problems develop.

That's where the vows come in. They say, "for richer or for poorer." The words are sentimental and poetic but must be accepted as a covenantal agreement. On their wedding day, every couple agrees to create their financial future together and embrace whatever that becomes, even if it is extreme. They say to each other, "If I'm poor, you are the one I want with me. If I'm rich, I do not want anyone else by my side. I want to be with you, whether it is steak and lobster or beans and franks. No matter what my status is in life, I know who I want." Yeah, that is love and marriage right there.

> The words are sentimental and poetic but must
> be accepted as a covenantal agreement.

The topic of money suggests another important point in the marriage contract. I mentioned much earlier in the book that each individual in the marital relationship has a function. Husband and wife are not simply labels or titles; they are functional roles. Each couple decides how they will function and what their roles will entail. Scripture indicates that the wife is the husband's financial responsibility. The old preacher would say that God gave Adam purpose and the ability to provide before He gave him a wife. What that means is man should be able to take care of the family he creates. While we know that in our society, the majority of households require two incomes, men should always remember that their wives are their God-given financial responsibility. The flip side is that a wife agrees to the financial capabilities of the husband when she accepts his marriage proposal. Sis, if he does not make enough money for you to be content, then just say no. It is unfair to stress your husband about something you knew about when he was just your boyfriend. But Sir, do not overextend yourself financially when you are dating in order to impress a woman. You should not pretend to be a big baller, giving her whatever her heart desires if your income cannot sustain it. Let there be truth in spending. It is important that she has the right information to determine if the lifestyle you provide is acceptable to her.

Which brings us back, once more, to the importance of proper dating, and, more specifically, proper marriage preparation once a couple is engaged. Again, couples should gather pertinent information about each other during the dating and engagement process, including financial information. There may have to be several awkward yet necessary conversations. Marriage is a merger; therefore, full financial disclosure is necessary. There are questions that have to be answered, such as how much debt each person has. What are the average monthly expenses and incomes? Are there any tax liabilities or liens? Is there back child support owed? Are there business investments? Is there a plan to quit a job to launch a business? Is there a plan to get another degree? Is there life insurance? These questions along with others have to be discussed in order to create and manage marital expectations so that money matters do not kill the marriage. Yes, I know those can be difficult, even embarrassing conversations. Many of us have had severe financial struggles. Our personal balance sheets do not balance, and we have more liabilities than assets. There are also those on the opposite extreme. They are wealthy and fear completely disclosing how rich they are. They want to know that their mate does not simply want them for their money. There is an element of fear on both sides. The poor, the middle class, and the just not rich are afraid their partner will reject them because of their financial situation, and the rich fear having a partner who is in love with the money. But, you have to be honest and upfront, even if it is hard.

Not only should you be upfront in general, you should be upfront even if it is at a difficult moment. Once people get engaged, usually they do not want to have conversations that could potentially stop the wedding. Once a proposal has been posted to numerous social media platforms and the bride-to-be has started flashing her ring, couples have a tendency to stay away from anything that could stop the big day. People begin to censor their words and monitor their personal exchanges. To those of you who are on the extremes regarding your finances, you cannot avoid the conversation and the truthful disclosure out of fear. Anything that can stop your wedding can later destroy your marriage. Engage in the conversations so that each partner can make an informed decision about getting married. You want both parties to commit without reservation to each other, so you can take the vows to be together for richer or for poorer and know the marriage can survive either extreme.

IN SICKNESS AND IN HEALTH

Wow! That is a tough one, but it is what every married couple signs up for. And, we are not done yet! From the very general "for better or for worse," to the hypothetical issues of money and providing in "for richer or for poorer," we come at last to an issue that will definitely affect every marriage: sickness and health.

I remember seeing a commercial, I believe it was for a particular hospital. The story caught my attention. There was a couple that had been married for four years, and within that time, the husband was diagnosed with cancer. The wife never dreamt their lives would take such a drastic turn, but they endured his treatments together. She helped nurse her husband back to health.

Just the other day, I was at an NFL game. The Vikings beat the Jaguars. (Go Vikings!) During one of the breaks, a wounded military veteran was honored. We all stood and gave him a standing ovation. He was in a wheelchair. His wife wheeled him out to the end zone to receive his honor. The public address announcer told the soldier's story. I wondered about the details of the couple's story since his injuries. With as many injured vets as there are in this country, I have to believe that all those spouses who stuck around to help them are heroes as well.

One more story. Let me tell you about one of my heroes and mentors, Dr. James E. Huger. Dr. Huger is an icon in the city of Daytona Beach, where I resided for over 25 years. His contribution to the city is immeasurable, and he had a tremendous impact on my life, ministry, and career. He created opportunity for me. He secured space for me in places I could have never reached on my own. God used him greatly in my life. He passed away on October 14, 2016 at 101 years young. On October 22, I had the honor of giving the benediction at his homegoing celebration. His wife, Mrs. Phannye Mae Brinson Huger, preceded him in death. Ms. Phannye was ill for some time before making her final transition on March 21, 2009.

This amazing couple dated for five years and was married for 67 years. While in his nineties, Dr. Huger was still active in Ms. Phannye's care. He would attend our 8 a.m. service at Hope Fellowship Church and ask to be excused prior to the benediction because he had to get back to his wife.

Dr. Huger embodied the true nature of his vow to be with his wife "in sickness and in health." They had many wonderful, healthy years. But, when Ms. Phannye's health went south, he was there. As couples grow older, health issues arise as the body ages. That's inevitable. That's going to happen.

On their wedding day, all couples (not just the extraordinary ones like those mentioned above) promise to be there for each other in sickness and in health. A healthy spouse is at full strength to support and cater to his or her partner. A spouse with a serious illness cannot. Severe health challenges can negate one's ability to fully function in the marriage. I once heard a woman give her testimony concerning her loving husband. She was a cancer victim and because of the illness and the type of medication she was taking, she could not have sexual intercourse for over two years. Her husband accepted their new reality and stuck by his wife. That is amazing! I do not mean for this section to be a downer. Many couples go through their entire marriage without any significant health challenges for either partner, at least until the end. I simply want to remind you of the breadth of the marital commitment.

Let me say something to the fellas right quick. Men are visual. Before we ever talk to a woman, we see her physical beauty and we become attracted. Initially, her physical appearance may be the sole reason we approach her. But, this vow tells you that is not going to be enough. Her face and figure cannot be the number one reason you marry her. Sickness can damage her appearance temporarily or permanently. She will need to know that you are still crazy about her because you love the rest of her as well.

Now, I realize that I have only addressed the possibility of physical sickness. This book is not long enough to cover all the ways couples deal with illness. Mental illness is prevalent and progressing in this country. There is also alcohol and drug addiction. I have seen firsthand some of the horror and heartbreak that families go through on that account. I have also witnessed some tremendous victories over addiction, and couples who were able to save and stabilize their marriage. Spiritual sickness has not been covered either, even if marriages are affected daily by a spouse's refusal to get saved, healed, and delivered from a sinful trait or tendency. Suffice it to say that all illness is not physical. All of these forms of sickness are realities. People face them every day. The point remains the same. If you get married, you vow to stick with your spouse through any of the above struggles. It's right there in the words.

Before I finish here, I would like to make a couple of additional points concerning marriage and physical health. The first is the effect that healthcare costs can have on your budget. They can take you from richer to poorer in a hurry. Do yourself a favor and practice good physical fitness and preventive health maintenance. If both partners commit to healthy living, it significantly decreases the chance that the "sickness" part of the vows will need to be tackled.

My final point is a little sensitive, so please hear me with the right ear and read my words with correct eye. I mean no offense but want to give you something to consider. In Chapter One, I made a case for marriage. I want to add to my argument. I want to raise the issue of the knowledge of family medical history. We have all had to fill out those dreaded medical history papers when seeing a new physician. There are myriad questions that ask you if particular diseases have affected your family line. I, for instance, always have to indicate that my father is diabetic and my mother has high blood pressure. So many people in my community either do not know their father or have no connection with him, so they consequently do not have knowledge of his medical history. Many people have no idea what physical illness run in their family, or if there is a history of mental illness. When an individual does not know, then it is impossible for a potential spouse to know. And it is best that both parties know. So, a little investigating can do wonders, and after that, a little honesty. Knowledge could save a life and even a marriage. You owe that to yourself, and to your spouse.

Honesty is key to all of these vows, of course. We need to honestly assess our partners and ourselves to make sure we are ready for the X Games that will be our marriage. We can never be sure what life has in store for us, whether we will get more than our share of positive extremes or more than our share of negatives. All we can do is be honest with one another and live by the promises we make at the altar. That way, we know for certain that even as we go through the unsafe years of marriage, we have a safety net underneath. We will have a partner we know will stick by us, and we know we'll also stick around. That way, we'll always be heading towards "better" even in the midst of the "worse."

REVIEW

1. How do the three vows in this chapter go from general to specific?

2. Why is honesty so important when it comes to money and health?

3. What does the story of Zipporah tell us about a spouse helping their husband or wife in moments of spiritual crisis?

SOUL SEARCHING

1. How can you prepare not just for the best days ahead but the worst in your marriage?

2. How does God help ease some of the difficulties of marriage? Do you feel that both you and your spouse (or potential spouse) are equally committed to God?

3. What kind of lifestyle do you expect from life? Do you have a partner who can help you reach that? If not, what is going to change, your expectations or your partner?

To Love and to Cherish

Considering the long journey the marriage vow takes us on, it's appropriate that it ends with concluding thoughts that pithily sum up everything. What we are asked to do, what we are promising to do at the altar, might be most simply put as: "to love and to cherish" and "till death do us part," before reminding us that this is "God's holy ordinance" and that we "plight," or promise, our partners our faith.

That is the whole vow in miniature. That is marriage at its very core: love forever with God at the center. So, to end this book, we will look closely at what each part of these concluding vows means.

TO LOVE

On their wedding day, the bride and groom promise to love each other. We all know that, and we take that point for granted. The question I would like to pose, though, is: How do we know what each individual means when they make this promise? What do the soon-to-be husband and wife mean when they say "I love you?" What kind of love do they promise to give each other? What is the exact intent of the vow itself?

Of course, we can draw a reasonable conclusion about the intent of the vow as written in the *Book of Common Prayer*, but the language lets us down somewhat here. Unlike the Greek of the New Testament, English lacks the nuance to properly explain an important concept like "love." We have to remember that these vows, as great as they are, are not scripture. They were written by Englishmen, in English, for English speakers, in 1549. If the vows were derived from scriptural text, we could go back to the original and do a word study to get the meaning. There are so many tools used to do word studies for scripture, starting with a simple Strong's Concordance. With those tools, we could break down exactly what the author meant because New Testament Greek can be so much more specific on these points than English.

When you do a simple word study on the world "love" in the New Testament, you find out that every time the word is used in the English translation of scripture, it does not necessarily come from the same Greek word, and does not mean the same thing.

For example, in John 21:15-20 there is a conversation between Jesus and Peter. Jesus asked Peter, "Do you love me…?" Peter responds, "Lord, you know that I love you." That seems like a simple affirmation of love between the two, but that impression is misleading. In the original Greek, Peter and Jesus use different words for love in their verbal exchange. Jesus asks for the selfless love of *agape* while Peter offers only *philia*, which is closer to friendship. Peter is falling short of what Jesus is asking him for, which will lead to his denial later. Of course, every Greek speaker would see the difference and understand immediately. It is only because of the translation that we miss it.

With that kind of obscurity built into our language, I think it is quite possible that, when two people repeat the marriage vow and commit to love each other forever, they could be repeating the same phrase while meaning completely different things. When two people stand at the altar and the preacher asks, "Do you promise to love?" and they say, "Yes," how do you know what they mean? Are the bride and groom saying the same thing when they say "I love you"?

C.S. Lewis in his classic, *The Four Loves*, describes four distinct types of love. They are affection, friendship, romance, and charity. For the church people who want to sound really deep, they are *storge, philia, eros,* and *agape.* As you can see, the Greeks had these distinctions all built into their language already. At the altar, they'd know right away if someone promised *philia,* while the other was promising *eros.* They'd know they weren't understanding each other. And that's an important point to catch, since each type of love is different in meaning, expression, and capacity, and each carries with it different expectations.

> … each type of love is different in meaning, expression, and capacity, and each carries with it different expectations.

So, what is the difference? Romantic love and friendship love are self-explanatory. According to Lewis, affection (*storge*) is the love one has for family. Charity (*agape*) is sacrificial, unconditional love. As we saw in the passage above, it is the love that Christ has for us, and the love we all are to have for each other. Since affection, friendship, romance, and charity are all distinctly different types of love, can you imagine the imbalance and potential conflict in a relationship if each party possesses a different kind of love for the other and expresses it accordingly? Imagine having romantic desires for someone who only has friendship and family desires for you. No man wants to hear from the woman he's dating, "I love you like a brother." No woman wants to hear, "You're like a sister to me," from someone she sees as a potential spouse. No one who is trying to make a love connection wants to hear they are in the friendzone or family-zone.

Man, it can be a tough pill to swallow when feelings are not mutual! (Please excuse the exclamation point. I started having a flashback.) A person can have deep affection (*storge*) for you but no romantic or erotic desires. That is the family-zone. You can have a strong sexual connection (*eros*) with a person and like very little else about them. So many people have mistaken lust for love.

There are several different combinations of uneven love exchanges. All of them should be avoided. Unrequited feelings among friends is tough. The tension between *philia* and *eros* is never easy. It is much worse when two people ignore the imbalance and exchange vows without exchanging the same form of love.

The love between a husband and wife is meant to be reciprocal. Each spouse will express love differently but the love shared by the couple should be of the same kind. If two people are in love they should know exactly what kind of love it is. Both you and your partner should know the type of love both of you require and what you will be exchanging. When you give one type of love, you expect the same in return. You do not anticipate receiving something totally different. Yet, it is possible for someone to love you but not the way you love them or the way you need to be loved. I repeat, when someone says, "I love you," get them to say it in Greek. You need to know what they mean.

Since your potential spouse probably doesn't know Greek, a declaration of love may require some follow-up questions. What do you think would happen if your romantic partner said to you, "I love you," and you gave them one or more of the following responses:

"When did you discover you felt this way?" "Tell me what you mean when you say that." "Why do you love me and how will I always know you do?" "What should I expect from your love for me?" "When do you feel this love most?"

I am sure bae might be thrown off a bit, but it would be very important for you to listen closely to what they say. Once your partner recovered from the conversation, hopefully, he or she would require you to answer the same questions, so they know that your relationship will be one of mutual exchange of high-quality love complete with all the different strands.

And that point is key. Love should not be just one form or another. For a relationship as important, intense, and long-lasting as marriage, no eliminations or substitutes will do. Affection and friendship are not adequate responses to romantic gestures. Romance, sex, or erotic behavior alone will never compensate for the absence of affection, friendship, and charity. I am amazed at the number of people who believe sexual chemistry and satisfaction is sufficient for marital longevity and contentment.

The truth is, although each type of love varies in its value, you cannot have a successful marriage without all four kinds of love being present.

As I mentioned above, Lewis says affection (*storge*) is family love. If we make a study of the word "family," we find that one of its derivatives is familiar. Familiarity alone is not a solid foundation for marriage, but it is how some people end up together. "Well, you know, we were just hanging out, and we get along, so we figured we'd go on and do it." "I'm comfortable with him. He is comfortable with me." Familiar. Like family, the people you are comfortable seeing every day. On the surface, that seems like it should be a good enough foundation for a marriage, but without those other elements, the relationship can quickly fall apart. So, when the person stands at the altar and you say "I love you," and they say "I love you" back, are they talking about indiscriminate familiar affection?

I'm not saying familiar is necessarily bad. Sometimes, marrying the familiar can work. Your perfect mate can be right around you for years, and you discover the treasure hidden in plain sight. In this case, all the other forms of love are there, they just showed up a bit late. Other times, however, fear and relationship fatigue can cause people to panic and settle for the familiar (and only the familiar). Have you seen one of those movies where two unmarried friends make an unusual pact? "If we are both single in five years, then we will get married. We are great friends. We get along well. The rest will come." I wish those stories were only in romantic comedies, but I have seen them become real life tragedies.

Of course, there's also a good reason that "familiar" is connected to "family." If you have followed the dating advice in Chapter Two, you are quite familiar with your future spouse's qualities, both positive and negative. You're comfortable with that person—that's a good thing. You trust they will be there every day, just like family. You need to be familiar, but that can't be it.

One of the other things a couple needs is friendship (*philia*). I'm not saying you need to be friends first, but you need to become friends at some point. Friendship in a romantic relationship is important. Commonality is critical. Marriage is about sharing, if it is about anything at all. Two people build a life and share it. Friendship gives you something to share—common interests, tastes, etc. Friends share but also help each other to grow. Their differences complement each other. Opposites do attract, but they do not always have what is necessary to remain attached. Ask yourself, *In our relationship, what do we have between us besides attraction?* Sooner or later, romance and/ or familiarity alone will not cut it. "I love you." "I love you too." "You love me?" "Yeah, I love you." "You're beautiful. You're handsome." Marriage is for life. You will not be able to spend all of your time being romantic. Romance massages attraction, develops appreciation, and stokes erotic flames. Friendship gives you something to do, and someone to enjoy being with when you are not being romantic.

But don't think that friendship alone will be enough either. Romance (*eros*) shouldn't be the only thing in a relationship, but it needs to be present. Yet, I have seen friends get married who had no genuine romantic attraction to each other. Romance is critical to a healthy marriage, especially in today's social media culture. Before the days of social media, men and women had to contend with the beautiful romantic images portrayed in magazines, in movies, and on television. Now, the romantic escapades of the rich and famous (and not so rich and famous) are minute-by-minute plastered all over the myriad of social media platforms. It is hard to compete these days if you are not romantic.

It is important here to be distinct in the meaning of words. When I say *eros* is necessary, I am not just talking about sex. I am talking about romance because when the Bible speaks of *eros* or the "erotic," it is not just talking about sex either. As a matter of fact, in Greek mythology, Eros (or, as you might know him, Cupid) was not sex, Eros was romance. Venus was sex. Many confuse Venus with Eros. As mentioned in the first part of Chapter Seven, sex is also important to a marriage, but it is not the whole of the romance (just as romance is not the whole of love) that needs to exist in a healthy marriage. We need some Venus, but we need more Eros.

Too many people confuse great sex with good love. Just as people confuse Eros with Venus. Eros can lead to Venus, but the reverse does not often happen. Sex does not lead to romance.

Even if affection (*storge*), friendship (*philia*), and romance (*eros*) are all present, a marriage still requires something else to function. *Agape* is pivotal. The *agape* love, or charity, that we are to possess for one another is delineated in 1 Corinthians 13:4-8. The requirements of love described in these verses are what we should all strive to meet in every type of interpersonal relationship. While not limited to romantic relationships, this quality of love is paramount to a lasting marriage. Anyone planning to get married should become very familiar with these verses.

Love [agape] is patient, love is kind. It does not envy, it does not boast, it is not proud. It is not rude, it is not self-seeking, it is not easily angered, it keeps no record of wrongs. Love does not delight in evil but rejoices with the truth. It always protects, always trusts, always hopes, always perseveres.

Love never fails... (1 Corinthians 13:4–8, NIV84).

Every time I read these scriptures, I think about the many occasions I still fail to live up to the standard of love found in them. I keep trying with the help of God. The verses really need no commentary. They are plain and straightforward. I can remember trying to develop an expository sermon using them as the text. There was really nothing to develop. The verses say what they mean, and the overall meaning is that *agape* love is what you give and not what you feel.

Let's go back to the question of why you love your partner. Many love their partner because of the contribution their mate makes to them. He understands me. She supports me. He is attentive. She is sensitive to my needs. They love because of all the *storge, philia,* and *eros* they receive.

But, marriage is a lifetime of giving as well as receiving. As a matter of fact, *agape* love is giving without the requirement to receive. God through Jesus Christ is the perfect example. God loves us sacrificially and expects us to do the same for each other. Since marriage is the primary adult human relationship, sacrifice should be a part of the foundational and operational mix of marriage.

> God loves us sacrificially and expects
> us to do the same for each other.

At the very beginning of this book, I said that marriage is not for selfish and self-centered people. Let me emphatically say it again. It is not for selfish and self-centered people. It also is not for the undisciplined and emotionally immature. Read the verses again.

Love is patient, love is kind. It does not envy, it does not boast, it is not proud. It is not rude, it is not self-seeking, it is not easily angered, it keeps no record of wrongs. Love does not delight in evil but rejoices with the truth. It always protects, always trusts, always hopes, always perseveres (1 Corinthians 13:4–7, NIV84).

To live happily ever after will require that type of love. Yet, to the surprise of some Christians, *agape* love alone is not enough either. Some would say that if you simply follow 1 Corinthians 13 you will have a great marriage. I say they are wrong unless they are operating under the presupposition that all of the other love variables are in place. There will be times when *agape* love is the only love that keeps the relationship from failing. Nevertheless, I need to say, especially to Christians, that while *agape* love is important to a marriage, it is not singular in its import. A good marriage will require a blend of all four forms of love: affection, friendship, romance, and charity; *storge, philia, eros,* and *agape.* Each type of love is significant, and none of them alone is a sufficient foundation to build a marriage, not even *agape.* When two people promise to love on their wedding day, hopefully, they mean love in all of its forms. That kind of love is big, deep, wide, and robust.

So how do partners know what each other means when they say "I love you"? The answer is in their actions. Love is defined by what your partner gives in the relationship. Words are great but can be suspect. Actions are more definitive. Hopefully, you have never been told or had to tell someone, "You don't love me the way I love you." That statement articulates an obvious difference and disconnect between two people and the type of love they have for one another. How do they know how you love them? It is called relationship experience. "Love" is a verb. Love is what it does. It is not measured according to the depth of feelings. Your lover can have an intense emotional attachment to you and treat you like crap. You know, the person who goes completely off the rails if you break up because they cannot bear to lose you but constantly ignores or disrespects you throughout the relationship. He or she loves you deeply but does not love you well. Your mate can have plenty of the wrong kind of love for you, a heart full of inferior love.

I say again, love should be a mutual exchange with varied expression. Once you have been dating for a while, you should have a preview of how some of the relationship dynamics will play out in the marriage. If you are not being loved the way you desire, fix it before the wedding day. There are no miracles at the altar. It is what it is. You have to make sure it is what you desire.

TO CHERISH

The purpose of this book has been to help couples in their marital preparation by giving emphasis and more in-depth meaning to the traditional wedding vows. The premise of the book is my presupposition that many, if not most, people pay very little attention to the meaning, covenants, conditions, and obligations of marriage set forth in the wedding vows. I know I didn't on June 10, 1989, as I stood at that altar in a beautiful ceremony, repeated the vows, and initiated a marriage that would ultimately end in divorce. I wish someone had shared with me what I have attempted to share with you in this book, especially this next word: "cherish." Or, better yet, I wish that I would have paid more attention and done more research.

If we go on dictionary.com, the basic definition of the word "cherish" is "to feel love for; to hold or treat as dear." But, that is only a part of the definition. The broader connotation of the word is to care for tenderly, to nurture, to cling to and protect. To cherish is to have such a deep feeling about something or someone that the feelings lead to actions of perpetual care and protection. To say that I cherish something says there is a feeling that I have about someone or something that causes me to protect him, her, or it.

There are certain things you own or possess to which you give sanctuary. They are not for general, public consumption. Maybe the item is very expensive, but that is not a requirement for it to be cherished. Maybe you treasure it because it was a gift from a special person or has a special memory attached to it. Some things are valuable not because of how much they cost but because of who gave them to you or who they remind you of. You protect them because they are irreplaceable to you and to lose them would cause you emotional pain. The more you value something, the better you care for it, and the more you protect it. There is a story in the Bible, in Luke 15:8-10, of a woman who lost a valuable coin. The coin was one of a set of coins, possibly a part of a wedding garland. The woman swept her entire house until she found the missing coin because she cherished it so much.

> The more you value something, the better you
> care for it, and the more you protect it.

When taking the traditional wedding vows, brides and grooms promise to cherish one another. To cherish involves two dimensions. You cherish your spouse, and you cherish the relationship. The individuals within the couple love, nurture, care for, cling to, and protect each other and the relationship. I know that is the intent in almost every marriage. But, the vow makes it more than an intent. It makes it a promise. When you get married, in essence, you tell your spouse, "You can count on me to cherish you and this relationship." You feel so strongly about your partner and about your relationship that you put them both in your protective custody. You care for, nurture, and protect them because you do not want the unbearable pain of losing them.

In my first marriage, I loved, but I did not cherish. That was a huge mistake. I had deep, intense feelings for her, but those feelings did not lead me to put both her and the relationship in protective custody. I thought I cherished the person, and to a much lesser degree, cherished the relationship. As I look back with better lenses, I realize I pretty much failed on both counts. I loved deeply, but I did not love well. If I had truly cherished either her or the relationship, I would have ended up caring for and protecting the other by default. If I nurtured and cared for her, I would have handled the relationship differently. I nurtured my children. I cleaved to my ministry career. And, most importantly, I protected my ego. Because of it, I did not humble myself, pray, and get help to solve the necessary issues. The reason I continue to say that marriage is not for the selfish and self-absorbed is because I was both and did not even know it.

When you cherish a person you care for, you nurture and protect them. I know I am being redundant with those words and phrases, but I do not know if we can say them enough. I think it is an amazing thing to love and actively care for someone so much that you can say to them, "If I ever hurt you, it will be a mistake, not an error or bad judgement, but a real mistake."

When you cherish your relationship, you protect it. You keep it from harm. You do not let anything get in the way of it because you know to lose it will be painful. You know you love it so much, you do not want to injure it, even if it means sacrificing yourself for the good of the relationship. As always, God is the consummate example. In perhaps the most famous line in all of scripture, John 3:16 says, *"For God so loved the world, that he gave his only begotten Son, that whosoever believeth in him should not perish, but have everlasting life"* (KJV). He sacrificed Himself in order to salvage His relationship with us. If He doesn't pay for our sins, He can't have His preferred type of relationship with us. So, since He wants that relationship with us, He pays for all the sins of a sinful humanity. Husbands, that is why the Apostle Paul compares your relationship with your wife to Jesus' relationship to the church.

Wives, submit to your husbands as to the Lord. For the husband is the head of the wife as Christ is the head of the church, his body, of which he is the Savior. Now as the church submits to Christ, so also wives should submit to their husbands in everything.

Husbands, love your wives, just as Christ loved the church and gave himself up for her to make her holy, cleansing her by the washing with water through the word, and to present her to himself as a radiant church, without stain or wrinkle or any other blemish, but holy and blameless. In this same way, husbands ought to love their wives as their own bodies. He who loves his wife loves himself. After all, no one ever hated his own body, but he feeds and cares for it, just as Christ does the church—for we are members of his body. "For this reason a man will leave his father and mother and be united to his wife, and the two will become one flesh." This is a profound mystery—but I am talking about Christ and the church. However, each one of you also must love his wife as he loves himself, and the wife must respect her husband (Ephesians 5:22–33, NIV84).

In order for Jesus to present the body to Himself, He had to save it. To save it, He had to sacrifice Himself. When you cherish the person and the relationship, you sacrifice yourself to save it because you trust the fact that the person you hooked up with is going to do the same for you. If you love and cherish your spouse and your relationship, care for them and nurture them even when there is conflict.

It is during conflict that we often stop caring. When we temporarily or momentarily stop caring, we can leave our partner or our relationship exposed to danger or injury. Any enemy to your marriage will try to capitalize on the opening. You have seen these common scenarios play out. Your partner hurts, offends, or simply gets on your last reserve nerve. He or she says the wrong thing on the wrong day. You go for the jugular because every spouse knows where it is. You unnecessarily injure your spouse and potentially the relationship.

Then, someone else moves in to comfort you or your injured partner. Sis, you want your husband to be more attentive. Your male co-worker proves to be very attentive. Do you protect your relationship from your legitimate need for attention? Sir, your wife makes you feel inadequate. Another woman makes it clear that you are the best man she has ever met. Do you protect and nurture your relationship or your ego? The scenarios are endless and they are more real than we may want to admit. Conflicts are inevitable, and the right temptation can test your commitment. Those are factors that you cannot control. What you can control is your decision to remember you promised to cherish your spouse and your relationship even when it is difficult. The key to effective conflict management and resolution is to always separate the issue from the person when appropriate and to always put the relationship above the issue. Do not allow any issue to be more important than your relationship. Remember to love your spouse with all four types of love at all times and to cherish what you have with them. That is the safest way to avoid any temptations that come your way.

Wow! I just took a deep breath. Marriage requires a lot, a whole lot. You have to cherish something that demands so much from you. I hope you do, and I hope your partner does as well.

REVIEW

1. What are the four types of love?

2. Why do we need all four types to make a marriage work?

3. What does it mean to cherish a marriage?

4. How do you make sure you and your partner avoid future temptation?

SOUL SEARCHING

1. Can you see all four types of love in your partner's actions? Look at your own actions. Do you show your partner all four types as well?

2. Think of a cherished object. Why do you cherish it so much? Do you look at your future spouse and your relationship and feel that same love and concern?

3. Have you put your ego aside for your relationship? Do you cherish your relationship as much as you love your partner?

Till Death Do Us Part

Most of my childhood storybooks began with "once upon a time..." and ended with "...and they lived happily ever after." The good stories took me on suspenseful journeys between those two points, journeys that moved from peace and tranquility to danger and intrigue before moving back again. Even if the end was always the same, when hearing stories for the first time, I would fear for the safety of Little Red Riding Hood as she dealt with the big, bad wolf or Goldilocks as she encountered the three bears. I remember feeling so relieved to know that, in the end, all would be well, and the main characters would live happily ever after. A marriage tale should go something like this. Once upon a time, two people met, dated, built a relationship based on love (all four kinds!), got married, and lived happily ever after, till death parted them. Nevertheless, in the United States too often the last line of our proverbial wedding tale is not, "till death parted them." It is unfortunately, "The marriage failed and they parted ways."

Here are some numbers for you. We all know that famous statistic that 50 percent of marriages in the U.S. end in divorce, but break down those figures a little more and the facts are even more disturbing. According to the Center for Disease Control and Prevention, in

America in 2015, there were over 800,000 divorces (who better to keep track of such an issue?). That makes 66,667 divorces a month, 15,385 divorces a week, and 2,192 divorces a day. In fact, that means, somewhere in America, there are 1.5 divorces every minute. And that doesn't even include California, our most populous state, which doesn't report the number of divorces it sees!

... somewhere in America, there are 1.5 divorces every minute.

According to the U.S. Census Bureau in 2011, the average marriage that ends in divorce lasts just eight years.

Across the board, the evidence suggests those who get divorced once tend to struggle to stay married the next time. That means, those who fail at marriage once are increasingly likely to fail again, and again, and again. According to a Pew Research study in 2014, 40 percent of new marriages involve someone getting remarried, and there are over 42 million people in the U.S. who have remarried at least once. That is about 17 percent of U.S. residents, according to the U.S. Census Bureau. And, each one of those marriages is more at-risk for divorce.

This is just scratching the surface. There are numerous, very informative studies on marriage and remarriage for those who like to plow through the numbers. But, I warn you, the information can seem pretty bleak.

Many people combine these stats with their own personal horror stories and conclude that, for most people, long-lasting, "till death do us part" marriages are, at best, a game of chance or, at worse, a fantasy that sounds good. I simply do not agree. The numbers are what they are. The terrible testimonies are what they are. But, marriage can work and should work more than it does.

As I have pointed out in several places, in this chapter and others, marriages are not successful on their own. Husbands and wives have to do the work, beginning with the dating process and then at every stage of the relationship that follows. If you date intelligently, choose wisely, thoroughly prepare, and fully commit to the relationship, your marriage can be a happy one and last forever. When two people repeat the vows of holy matrimony, they promise to remain united for life. They promise that only death will separate them—nothing else. The language reminds me of the verbiage of scripture in Romans 8.

Who shall separate us from the love of Christ? Shall trouble or hardship or persecution or famine or nakedness or danger or sword? (Romans 8:35, NIV84).

For I am convinced that neither death nor life, neither angels nor demons, neither the present nor the future, nor any powers, neither height nor depth, nor anything else in all creation, will be able to separate us from the love of God that is in Christ Jesus our Lord (Romans 8:38–39, NIV84).

I have always loved the resolve of those verses. Christ has determined that nothing shall separate us from his love. He has united us with his *agape* love and will let nothing come between to part us from it. He has taken responsibility for the security of the union. He decided to love us first, and He is resolved to keep loving us no matter what. Because His love is unconditional and He is the power over life and death, Jesus is truly able to make this a promise, not a wish, a hope, or mere sentimental statement.

We make a similar promise to our spouse when we get married. When we take the vow, we announce our decision and determination to not allow anything but death to separate, divide, sever, or split us up from our partner. Each partner commits to protect the unit from any and all instruments of division.

I have heard couples say, "Things just fell apart," or "We grew apart." I have heard wives say, "She came between us," and husbands say, "He came between us." The promise on the wedding day was to let nothing but death come between. Death is out of our hands. Death cannot be controlled. It takes whomever it pleases. It makes a wife a widow and a husband a widower, and there is nothing either can do. Every other instrument of separation can be controlled with the help of God. So, when couples fall apart, grow apart, or get divided, it means someone did not hold up their responsibility to fight off any and all instruments of division. I, too, am guilty as charged.

In the spirit of Romans 8:35, I ask these questions: What shall mentally, emotionally, or spiritually separate you from your spouse? Shall conflict or neglect, misunderstandings or unforgiveness? Shall lust or ego, career or ministry? Shall children, stepchildren, or any other person, feeling, deed, or emotion? All of these things, individually or in some combination, can separate a couple, if they are allowed to. It is up to each individual within the couple to protect the marriage from anything that would divide them. There has to be a sense of determination to let nothing separate you. Be strong and conquer every threat to your relationship unity "till death do you part."

I keep repeating that phrase, "till death do you part," because it is such strong language. While all of the phraseology of the wedding vows is poetic, that line is so ultra-formal. It sounds like something

James Earl Jones might say in one of his more philosophical roles. As I am writing, I can hear his voice saying the line. Can you imagine having to repeat your wedding vows after Mufasa or Darth Vader? The verbiage used in this line is just so formal. Of course, there are plenty of other ways to say it that are more romantic and less ominous. You could speak in terms of forever, or always, or forever and always, or always and forever. You could replace the line with "for the rest of my life," or, my personal favorite, "till I take my last breath." Regardless of your choice of words, they all come to mean the same thing: marriage is meant to be for a lifetime. Everyone should get married with that long view in mind. "For the rest of my life" is such romantic language. Forever is such a warm and fuzzy word. I define forever as every day until you die. My verbiage is not as pleasing to the ear in comparison, but the connotation is important to the long-term success of a marriage.

> "For the rest of my life" is such romantic language.
> Forever is such a warm and fuzzy word.

Marriages are meant to end at a cemetery and not a courtroom. Though marriage is a lifetime commitment, couples have to remember that life is lived one day at a time. Marriage, then, is a daily commitment to forever. Every day a true spouse makes a commitment to the longevity of his or her marital relationship. Every day matters, every day full effort should be made. A blissful day does not cause the couple to decrease their effort on the day following. Every day, each partner should love and cherish each other and the relationship by making the effort to meet each other's needs and expectations. Nothing should be taken for granted. There should be a daily commitment to forever, even on the bad days.

A long view of marriage gives proper perspective to the difficult days. When your perspective is that you will be together always, a painful day is not considered fatal. A difficult season is not perceived as the beginning of the end. Couples who are committed to forever accept the reality of potential hardship and misfortune in their relationship. They don't expect every day to be sunshine and sprinkles. They know marriage is an Xtreme sport. There will highs and lows, and occasionally, someone can get hurt. Sometimes, there won't be just pain; there will be injury. But, couples with a long view of marriage live with the assurance that, as long each partner has the appropriate character and strength, then *agape* love, prayer, hard work, and professional help when necessary, can restore and renew their marriage over time. Some relationship issues take longer than others to work out, and some injuries take longer heal. There are dark times in any marriage, but when two committed partners decide that nothing but death will separate them, there is always hope for brighter days ahead. I have known couples who went their separate ways because of circumstances they felt they just could not overcome. When the dust settled and hurt feelings were assuaged, they realized they gave up too soon. With their perspective clouded by intense pain, they limited their choices by their own ineptitude and decided to sever what could have been saved. Years of potential happiness together were forfeited.

They gave up their "till death do us part" over some temporary inconvenience. Don't let that be the case with you.

REVIEW

1. Which group has the hardest time staying married?

2. How many divorces are there per minute in America?

3. How does "till death do us part" help get over day-to-day marriage difficulties?

SOUL SEARCHING

1. Why is the divorce rate so high in this country?

2. Why do you think those who get remarried have such a higher risk of getting re-divorced?

3. Think about Romans 8, quoted above. How can Jesus' love help you love your spouse better?

Eleven

According to God's Holy Ordinances I Plight Thee My Faith

When two people get married, they observe a sacred sacrament instituted by God. Marriage is a holy ordinance, which means that it is set apart to honor God. When I was a child, I used to hear people, who were opposed to marriage but not against living together while in a sexual relationship, say, "It's just a piece of paper." I have actually heard that same sentiment expressed recently. Marriage is not just a piece of paper. The institution of marriage is so much more than the license issued by the government. It is two people entering into a covenant with each other and the God of the universe. The holy ordinance of marriage is so special to God that, in scripture, it is compared to the relationship between Christ and the church. The church is the bride of Christ and Jesus is the bridegroom. Marriage is truly a God thing. It is no coincidence that, usually, after the vows are exchanged in a wedding ceremony, a prayer of blessing is prayed. The hope is that God will be present in the marriage and that He would bless it so it may give him honor and bring a lifetime of joy to the bride and groom. Marriage is important to God, and I cannot stress enough, the intent of God is that marriage should be for life.

Part of what I hope you have gotten from this book is that it is so easy to throw around words without truly grasping their signification. "For life" is a short phrase, but it has huge implications. To publicly declare what you will do and with whom you will be united for the rest of your life is a significant step of faith in God and in another fallible human being. The iteration of the marital vows that I use in my ceremonies (and in this book) speaks directly to the ability to believe in a person so much that you want to embrace an unknown future with them, fully assured that they are the best person with whom to take this journey called life. The vow says you plight your faith to your partner. The language of this final line is florid, just like the previous phrase, "till death do us part."

"I plight thee my faith" is such ornate verbiage. The translation is, "I pledge my faith to you." When two people enter into this holy covenant, they place their faith in each other and make a commitment to forever: "till death do us part."

When you get married, you tie your hopes for your future to another person. Your faith is in your partner whom you love. Marriage, then, is the convergence of your faith, hope, and love: faith in partner, hope for your future together, and the *agape* love necessary to make forever a reality. Along with God and certain family members, your partner is the known constant in your life as you face every unknown variable in your future. Yet, your family members don't make a promise to you before God and at least two witnesses. When you take the vows, you say to your partner, "I trust you with me, and I take on the responsibility of your trust you are placing in me." Trust is central to the success of a marriage. As a matter of fact, marriage is a trust. It is the ultimate leap of faith. It is the "all in" spin of the wheel or roll of the dice. As I've said before, marriage is risky business, but the reward of a great marriage is worth it.

Marriage is worth the risk, and that risk can be minimized if you are willing to put the effort in. I have said it hundreds of times: there is nothing wrong with marriage, there is something wrong with us, the people who get married. Marriage itself is a great blessing. Two people becoming one is an amazing miracle. Those of us who have seen marital relationships work can testify to the beauty and blessing of a great marriage.

> Marriage is worth the risk, and that risk can be minimized if you are willing to put the effort in.

Of course, I have seen a lot of divorce in my lifetime. I have even endured my own divorce. But, I am healed. It took a lot of work, prayer, some therapy, and several years, but I am healed. During my recovery from my divorce, as part of my healing process, I intentionally (and often unintentionally) watched couples a lot. I will admit that, for some time, I had wedding ring envy. Wedding rings make a statement. They say that the person is attached, that they belong to someone. I missed that. In church, in airports, in shopping malls, and on the street, I watched for those rings, and I studied the married couples they belonged to. I analyzed their interaction and listened to how they communicated with each other. Did they maintain close proximity to each other? Did they hold hands? When they spoke to each other, I didn't care what they were saying. I wasn't eavesdropping. I paid attention to *how* they spoke to each other. Did they use kind, respectful tones? Were they at all playful with each other? How did they communicate when they were obviously frustrated? Regardless of how brief the encounter, it can be easy to see if people are respectful, loving, and caring to each other or if they are enjoying each other's company.

From that period of my life onward, I have paid particular attention to couples who have been married 25 or more years. Marriages that have reached a certain longevity intrigue me. I think there is a lot those couples can teach us, if we are willing to pay attention and learn. Recently, I saw an ABC News article (2016) about a couple, Vera and John Peterson, who had been married 77 years (Nicole Pelletiere, "Couple to celebrate 77th wedding anniversary..."). In the article, the wife stated, "It has been wonderful. I'm not saying that everything was all roses. There were a few thorns as always, and I think everyone has that. It can't be perfect, but we have to have give and take." That is simple advice from a woman who has been married 77 years!

Out of curiosity, as I was preparing to write this book, I looked through the Hallmark list wedding anniversary meanings and the gifts associated with them. Most of the meanings and the gift suggestions seem a bit arbitrary to me. Why is leather the gift for year three? Who wants wool at year seven? I would have made some exchanges and alterations, but what do I know? I don't have the Hallmark algorithm. The list stops at the diamond anniversary. That is 60 years! For the Petersons' 77 years, I guess you just give them a standing ovation.

I have not had the pleasure of meeting the Petersons, or giving them a standing ovation, but for years, I have been lucky enough to closely watch three wonderful couples who have been blessed with long-lasting, happy marriages. They are: Roosevelt and Mary Taylor, Fertnand and Orpah Tharpe, and John Archie and Dianne Brown. All three husbands served as deacons for many years in our church.

When I was the pastor, they served me and the church admirably. They are still a part of my life and my circle of counsel. I love them and depend on their wisdom. The Taylors have been married for almost 60 years, the Tharpes for 48 years, and the Browns for 44 years. They are all incredible people. I watch each couple particularly closely. I listen to them intently. I love the joy their marriages bring to each of them. Just like the Petersons, they are all quick to say that it has not been easy, but they would not trade it for anything. Deacon Brown calls his life with Dianne "a remarkable journey." We should all be so fortunate, but then, we'd all have to be willing to work that hard!

I am willing. I'm working hard every day to invest in forever with my wife. I look forward to every milestone along the way: 5 years, 10 years, 25 years, and every year after. On the day of my 50th wedding anniversary, I will be 98 years old. Do not laugh. It could happen. A couple of years ago, I hosted the 100th birthday party of one of my mentors. He was lucid, vibrant, and stylishly dressed, so I know 98 years can be reached.

For that anniversary, I'm going to have a major celebration. As I am imagining the party, I am planning for it to be quite a night for my family and friends—at least my friends who will still be around. I wonder what I will wear. Most likely, it will be a black custom tuxedo, a white custom shirt, and a black bowtie. I will have to spend a little time finding the shoes. They have to be perfect. I don't know who will be on the guest list. So much will have changed by then. There will be new generations of Tripletts that will have been added to the family. I know there will be a lot of great food and live classic jazz. My wife will be stunning as usual. She is not picky, but I better get her a great gift. After all, it will be the golden anniversary, 50 years since we said, "I do."

Biography

Derek Triplett is a speaker, writer, and change agent with over 27 years of experience in pastoral ministry. He is a radio and television personality known for his expert relationship coaching. Since leaving full-time church ministry, Triplett travels the country speaking, training, and coaching individuals, ministries, and organizations to live and operate at full strength.

He is the author of *When I Became a Man: A Perspective on Manhood, Life and Relationships* and *Walk With Me: Daily Wisdom From the Sharp Mind (and Sometimes Tongue) of Derek Triplett.*

He is the father of two adult children and the stepfather of two. He and his wife, LuAnne Sorrell Triplett, live in the Orlando, Florida area.